£2.50

foreword

Jean-Christophe and I go back a long way. We have been like brothers since we were both starting out in the cooking world, and there's a lot of mutual respect. When I first met him, he seemed like a man obsessed, with his food and where he was going ... and he's still like that.

Since he first hit the London stage he has really played to his own audience and now with his own group of restaurants and no one to clip his wings he is free to be himself and explore his exceptional talent.

He's a very honest person — what you see with Jean is what you get — but he is also very complex, and his honesty and complexity are reflected in his food.

Sometimes I worry that he has bitten off more than he can chew, but then he's still chewing ...

Marco Pierre White

D0337113

novel
your place or

Quadrille

SARAH
J'eliees
If a Kiss won't do
Hope my cooking will
as you need that
Love
Jean Christophe
20.8.00

li
mine?

cooking at home with restaurant style

Jean-Christophe Novelli with Sheila Keating
Photography by Jean Cazals

For the three women I love: my mum,
who is a better cook than me, my daughter
Christina, and Anzelle. JCN

Art Director: Mary Evans
Publishing Director: Anne Furniss
Editor & Project Manager: Lewis Esson
Design: Paul Welti
Photography: Jean Cazals
Production: Candida Jackson

First published in 1998 by
Quadrille Publishing Limited,
Alhambra House,
27–31 Charing Cross Road,
London WC2H OLS

Reprinted in 1999

Text © 1998 Jean-Christophe Novelli
& Sheila Keating
Photography © 1998 Jean Cazals
Design & Layout © 1998 Quadrille
Publishing Ltd

The rights of Jean-Christophe Novelli and Sheila
Keating to be identified as the Authors of
this Work have been asserted by them
in accordance with the Copyright,
Design and Patents Act 1988.

All rights reserved. No part
of this book may be reproduced, stored
in a retrieval system or transmitted in any form
or by any means, electronic, electrostatic, magnetic
tape, mechanical, photocopying, recording or otherwise,
without the prior permission in writing of the
publisher.

Cataloguing in Publication Data: a catalogue record for
this book is available from the British Library

ISBN 1 899988 18 1

Typesetting by Peter Howard
Printed and bound by Mohndruck Graphische Betriebe
GmbH, Germany

Note: nature is unpredictable, and so are
ovens, so it is impossible to be unequivocal
about cooking times. Your fish might be a
little thicker than mine, your quails' eggs
a little larger; I use gas, you might use
electricity ...

Remember, too, that no one ever became a
chef in a day, or stopped learning. The fun
of cooking is adapting, developing,
experimenting...

contents

author's preface

Suivant mon humeur — according to my mood, my passion — is the description that accompanies the dish of pigs' trotters on all my menus, a dish that is prepared in a different way each day. When critics write about my restaurants it is the thing they always pick up on, perhaps because it sums up my whole attitude to cooking, in fact my whole attitude to life.

For me nothing ever stays still. I am always searching for the next idea, the next adventure ... to stand still is to stagnate. Even while I am perfecting one dish I am already thinking of how I can take it one stage further, or take apart its elements and reassemble them in another dish. Even before I opened my first restaurant, in my mind I was already planning the next three.

People say to me, 'Slow down, you can't do all these things, take your time,' but I say, 'You don't know me'. I live my life through instinct, by trusting what my heart tells me to do, then throwing myself into a project, without sleep, without thinking about anything else, until it is perfect.

I am not completely crazy, however, I know that to have success you must have a foundation that is solid and sure. In my restaurants I need the people who have cooked with me and shared experiences over the years — people I can trust. The same principle holds with my cooking. I may have a reputation for taking risks with daring

combinations of flavours, but at the heart of my dishes are sure and tested recipes, built on the principles of flavour and texture and the true marriage of ingredients. Once I have these recipes, then I can take chances, play with new flavours, be extravagant.

To simple recipes that you could cook at home every day for the family, I add new sauces and garnishes to build up more elaborate dishes, refined and presented in restaurant style, which you can try for special occasions. When you have the confidence to experiment and improvise for yourself, that is when cooking becomes a real joy. I hope that this book will help you to begin simply, then let your imagination soar. That is what I do at my place; why not try it at yours ... *suivant votre humeur.*

box of tricks

From a simple dish, many more can grow — variations, elaborations, whole families of dishes that can be served as starters or main courses. I think I am quite unusual in that when I first begin to think about a dish, I start with the shape, not the flavour. I sketch a design, and when I am happy with that, then I start to fill in the tastes and colours, building up the ideas until I have something that satisfies all the senses.

Often I will start with one of my trusted recipes, then I open up my box of tricks and add sauces, oils, powders and garnishes, as a child might experiment with building blocks. I love to watch people's faces when they see a dish, particularly a dessert, presented in a dramatic and unusual way, with springs made from caramel or a cigar-shaped tuile. Of course, the way a dish looks is only one element of its success. If something looks pretty, but tastes of nothing, what is the point? What we look for in most of our garnishes and decorative touches is that intensity of flavour which can be built up to give a dish three or four dimensions in terms of taste. Often the simplest techniques can do just that.

Imagine, you take two ingredients, basil leaves and some good olive oil, and you blitz them together. It takes — what? — two minutes, but the result is something so intensely flavoursome you wonder why you never used it before. We make many of our favourite oils and garnishes from things that other kitchens might discard: for example, instead of throwing away orange peel after you have taken the juice from the fruit, we make a powder with it for sprinkling on pan-fried scallops or plainly cooked fish. What does it cost? Nothing. From that humble ingredient you can create a little bit of magic. You might think it is a lot of work to turn orange peel into a concentrated powder, but what do you really have to do? You just blanch and dry the peel, dust it with a little salt and icing sugar and leave it in the oven on as low a setting as possible for a few hours until the moisture has all disappeared. Then you blitz it in a food processor. To make dried fruit or tomato or aubergine slices for eye-catching decoration you follow a similar process.

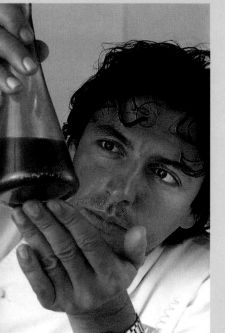

I think what sometimes makes the difference between the professional kitchen and the home kitchen is this emphasis on concentrated flavours. As a chef you season constantly, by instinct, but you also spend time reducing sauces again and again until you are left with pure intensity of flavour. The sauces don't have to be complicated: just to reduce some fresh orange juice to a syrup gives an extraordinarily powerful flavour, as does reducing some aged balsamic vinegar.

For me, oils, juices, reductions and powders are extra condiments, which can heighten the taste sensation of a dish instantly, and you will find them cropping up again and again in the recipes that follow. The beauty of them is that they can mostly be put together in advance and kept in the fridge or the store cupboard. They then form the basis of a valuable box of tricks that you can open at any time. Perhaps you are grilling a piece of fish, then why not drizzle around some concentrated sun-dried tomato juice and finish with a garnish of dried tomato? Instantly you have something that will taste and look a little different, just that bit more impressive.

Finally I should mention stocks and *jus,* which chefs make every day and take for granted. We prepare meat stock in the classic way by simmering roasted bones over a long time with aromatic vegetables. Fish stock is made by simmering bones, trimming and herbs for only about 20 minutes, otherwise it will become bitter. I recommend you make your own stock — partly because it is a very satisfying thing to do (I haven't given recipes in this book as I am sure you can readily find them elsewhere). If you don't have time, look for a good-quality ready-made variety. Where *jus* is mentioned, this is stock reduced down to the consistency of a sauce, which can then be combined with other ingredients or simply drizzled over a dish to add an extra dimension of intense flavour.

oils & reductions

Orange and Cardamom Reduction

It is amazing what depth and intensity of flavour you can get from simply reducing fresh orange juice in a pan with some cardamom pods very very slowly until it becomes thick and syrupy. This reduction adds a vibrant flavour to simple grilled fish, but I have also used it in all sorts of other ways: I have poured it over a dish of puréed carrots, then glazed this under the grill, or I have used it (without the garlic) as a syrup for poaching fruit like apples to serve with pain perdu (see page 156).

You could even push some vanilla pods through the centre of some bananas, dip them in the orange reduction (again without the garlic), then roast them briefly in the oven and serve them with some crème pâtissière, sandwiched between two layers of puff pastry.

makes about 50 ml

300 ml freshly squeezed orange juice
4 cardamom pods
1 garlic clove, split

1 Pass the orange juice through a fine sieve into a pan and add the cardamom pods and garlic.
2 Reduce very slowly until thick and syrupy. Leave to cool and store in the fridge.
3 Bring to room temperature before serving.

Orange, Vanilla and Cardamom Infused Oil

makes about 300 ml

300 ml freshly squeezed orange juice
4 cardamom pods
1 garlic clove, split
½ vanilla pod
250 ml extra-virgin olive oil

1 Make the orange and cardamom reduction as left.
2 While the reduction is still warm, mix in the seeds from the vanilla pod and the olive oil.
3 Leave for 24 hours to infuse.

Herb Oil

I often add this to mashed potatoes with a little cream and butter.

makes about 250 ml

1 bunch of basil, coriander or chives
250 ml extra-virgin olive oil

1 Dip the herbs in boiling water for 1 second, refresh in iced water and drain.
2 Put through a blender, then drizzle in the olive oil a little at a time until well blended.
3 Strain through muslin.

Chorizo Oil

makes about 1 litre

1 litre extra-virgin olive oil
1 chorizo sausage, thinly sliced
4 garlic cloves, crushed
4 bay leaves
2 sprigs of rosemary
2 sprigs of thyme
freshly ground salt and black pepper

1 Fry the chorizo and garlic gently in a little oil.
2 Stir in the herbs and season.
3 Transfer to a sterilized screw-top jar and cover with the rest of the oil. Keep for at least 24 hours and up to 2 weeks before use.

Sherry Dressing

makes about 350 ml

250 ml olive oil
3 tbsp sherry vinegar
1 tbsp clear honey
1 tsp grainy mustard
1 garlic clove, crushed
freshly ground salt and pepper

Combine all the ingredients together with 2 tablespoons of water and season to taste. Store in the fridge for up to 3–4 days.

Sun-dried Tomato Juice

makes about 1.5 litres

200 g shallots

1½ heads of garlic

20 ripe tomatoes

2 red peppers

115 g sun-dried tomatoes

50 g basil leaves

25 g thyme leaves

25 g tarragon

50 g unrefined caster sugar

100 ml white wine vinegar

500 ml water

freshly ground salt and pepper

1 Peel and slice the shallots and garlic. Slice the fresh tomatoes and peppers.

2 Put all of these in a pan with the sun-dried tomatoes, herbs, sugar, vinegar and water. Season. Bring to the boil and simmer for 10 minutes.

3 Take from the heat, cover and leave in a warm place for 12 hours.

4 Sieve into a clean bowl through muslin, allowing it to filter through without forcing. The juice can be bottled and refrigerated for 2-3 days.

Red Pepper Reduction

makes about 50 ml

500 g bright red peppers, chopped

20 g unrefined caster sugar

1½ tbsp white wine vinegar

1 Whiz the peppers with 3½ tablespoons water in a blender to a purée. Squeeze through muslin or a fine sieve.

2 Stir in the sugar and vinegar. Put in a pan and bubble up until reduced to a syrup.

3 Allow to cool and chill. Bring to room temperature before serving.

dried fruit & vegetable slices

It takes a little practice to find the right timings for your oven.

for Dried Aubergine or Carrot Slices:

Slice the aubergine or carrot thinly at an angle, to produce oval-shaped slices about 2 mm thick. Lightly grease 2 sheets of baking paper with butter, then sprinkle with sea salt (this helps to draw out the moisture from the vegetable).

Place 1 of the sheets of baking paper on a baking tray and lay the vegetable slices on top. Cover with the second sheet of paper (this will keep the slices flat). Put into the oven on the lowest possible setting for about 2 hours, until completely dried out and crisp.

for Dried Tomato Slices:

Slice the tomatoes across about 2 mm thick and then follow the method for dried aubergine or carrot, leaving for about 4 hours.

for Dried Celeriac Slices:

Slice the celeriac thinly, about 2 mm. Heat a little olive oil in a frying pan and fry the celeriac slices briefly on both sides. Drain. Salt the slices and lay them between two sheets of baking paper on a baking tray. Put in the oven on the lowest possible setting for about 3 hours, until dry and crisp.

Dried Limes

Thinly slice your limes (about 2 mm), put on a non-stick tray and dust with icing sugar. Put in the oven at the lowest possible setting and leave for 2–3 hours until completely dried and crisp. You can also do this with slices of apple, orange or lemon.

Orange Powder

Pare off the rind of 10 oranges, remove any attached pith, and blanch the rind for 1 minute in boiling water. Refresh in cold water, drain and pat dry, then arrange on a non-stick baking tray. Sprinkle with salt and a little icing sugar, then dry in the oven on its lowest possible setting for 2–3 hours until crisp. Grind to a powder in a food processor and pass through a fine sieve. Store in an airtight jar until required.

Carrot Powder

Peel 6 large carrots, then grate them. Wrap the grated carrot in muslin and squeeze out excess juice. Spread the carrot out on a baking tray, sprinkle with salt and dry in the oven on its lowest possible setting for 2–3 hours until crisp. Grind to a powder in a food processor and pass through a fine sieve. Store as above.

Cep Powder

Clean the ceps and roughly chop them. Season with salt then place them on a baking tray. Leave in the oven on the lowest possible setting for 3–4 hours, until crisp. Grind to a powder then put through a fine sieve. Store as above.

A Note about Seasoning

One of the most important things a chef learns is how to season food correctly. Sometimes when people cook at home and are disappointed with the bland taste of a dish, I think it is because they have not been bold enough with the seasoning. Cooking is all about proportion and balance, and the use of salt and pepper is the basis of that. However, most recipes simply say 'add salt and pepper to taste', or 'add a pinch of salt', referring to seasoning once, perhaps twice, when a chef will automatically season at many stages.

Throughout the recipes in this book I have tried to point out the correct times to season. However, seasoning is something that

will come naturally when you cook the same dishes often enough. You get a feel for bringing the flavours through; after all, the idea of seasoning is to enhance the natural flavours of the food, not to be the dominant taste.

When cooking meat or fish, I would always salt it before cooking, otherwise as the meat or fish cooks it will become sealed on the outside, creating a wall against whatever seasoning you add to it, and preventing it from being absorbed properly into the flesh. With sauces I would season at the beginning of cooking, then taste and adjust as necessary at the end.

I only use unrefined rock or sea salt, because it brings out the flavours of food without adding an artificial saltiness. Before each service, it is crushed and placed in bowls, accessible to all the chefs. The pepper we use is a mixture of black and white peppercorns freshly crushed with a few coriander seeds in the Robocoupe to give a fine pepper which won't leave sauces looking speckled.

Deep-fried Herbs

When certain large-leaved herbs are deep-fried in vegetable oil they take on an intense colour and translucence, like stained glass. Basil and bay give the most stunning effects. The most important thing is to dip the leaves only briefly in the hot oil. As they are lowered in, they will crackle as their moisture comes in contact with the fat. The moment they stop crackling, remove them with a spider or slotted spoon and drain them on kitchen paper.

Caramel Springs

As Marco Pierre White is fond of reminding me, in cooking you cannot re-invent the wheel. You can only try to find and perfect different ways of combining and presenting ingredients. Well, I didn't invent caramel, of course not, but one day, when I was in the kitchen at Keith Floyd's pub in Devon, I accidentally discovered a way of working with it that I believe to be original.

I was making some caramel cages (very fashionable at the time) and I left my spoon in the pot to do something else. When I came back, I found a tiny thread of caramel wound around the handle of the spoon: it looked like a perfectly coiled spring. It was set hard and when I slid it off the handle, it kept its shape.

My problem was to reproduce it. I tried using the handle of a wooden spoon, but if the atmosphere was humid, the caramel would cling to the wood, so I tried drying out the spoon in the oven before using it. That didn't help. I tried winding the caramel around pens and every kind of cylinder I could find in the kitchen. Finally, I tried a knife-sharpening steel, which gave me the perfect spring: the diameter was just right, and its coldness set the caramel the moment it touched it.

Working with caramel requires understanding and patience. Unless, like me, you have a restaurant full of customers demanding it, it is not something to work with when you are in a hurry or a bad mood. And it is easiest to make on a cool day, as heat and humidity can make it damp and sticky to handle.

Like a steam train, the caramel process starts slowly, but when it gets up speed you have to be careful not to let it run away from you or the caramel will burn. The way to control it is to keep it at a gentle, steady pace.

We make caramel by heating unrefined caster sugar in a heavy-based pan (some people add liquid glucose, or a little water). We always use unrefined sugar as it has a more pure taste. As you heat the sugar slowly, it will turn first to a transparent liquid, then begin to colour and caramelize at about 150ºC. After that it will pass through a shade which is just darker than gold — take it from the heat quickly or it will colour rapidly and when it reaches around 190ºC will burn and taste bitter.

Always take care when working with caramel; if you splash yourself with it, it will keep its temperature after hitting your skin, causing a nasty burn.

Make your springs just before you need them, then you have to be quick. Take a spoon in one hand and hold a sharpening steel in the other. Dip the spoon into the hot caramel, then lift it out, pulling a thin thread of caramel after it. Quickly wind this five or six times around the steel, pulling the thread very slightly as you do so, so that the spirals are about 2 cm apart. The caramel will set almost instantly and, as it does so, slide the spring carefully from the sharpening steel and place on a sheet of baking paper folded up into a series of concertina folds until ready to use.

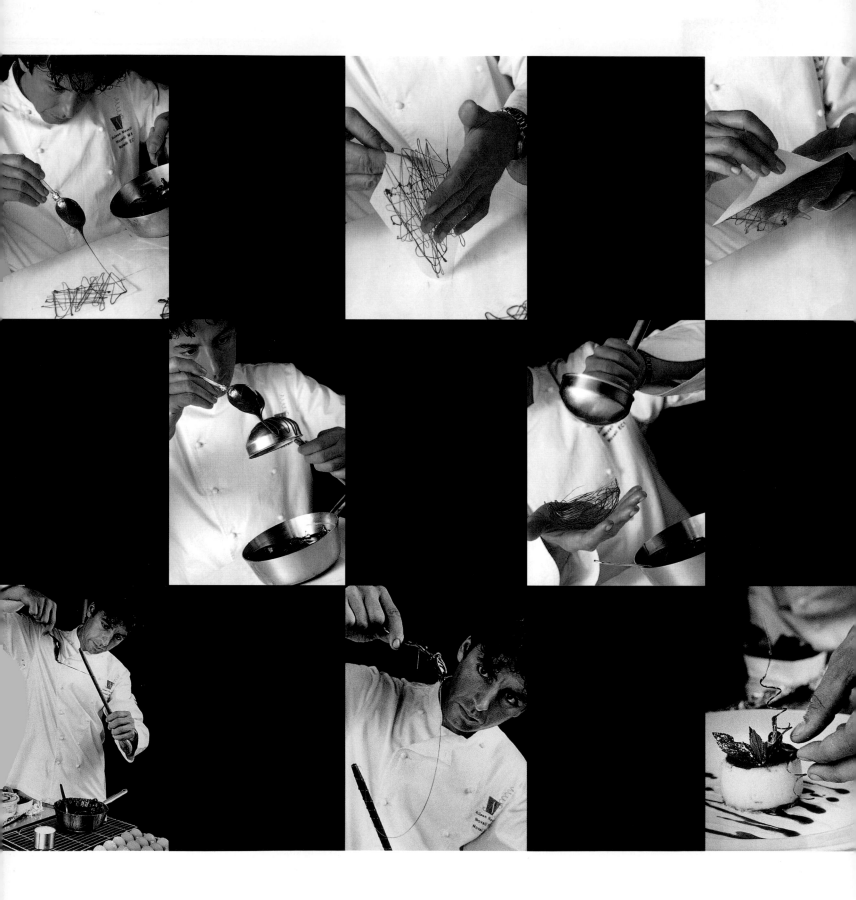

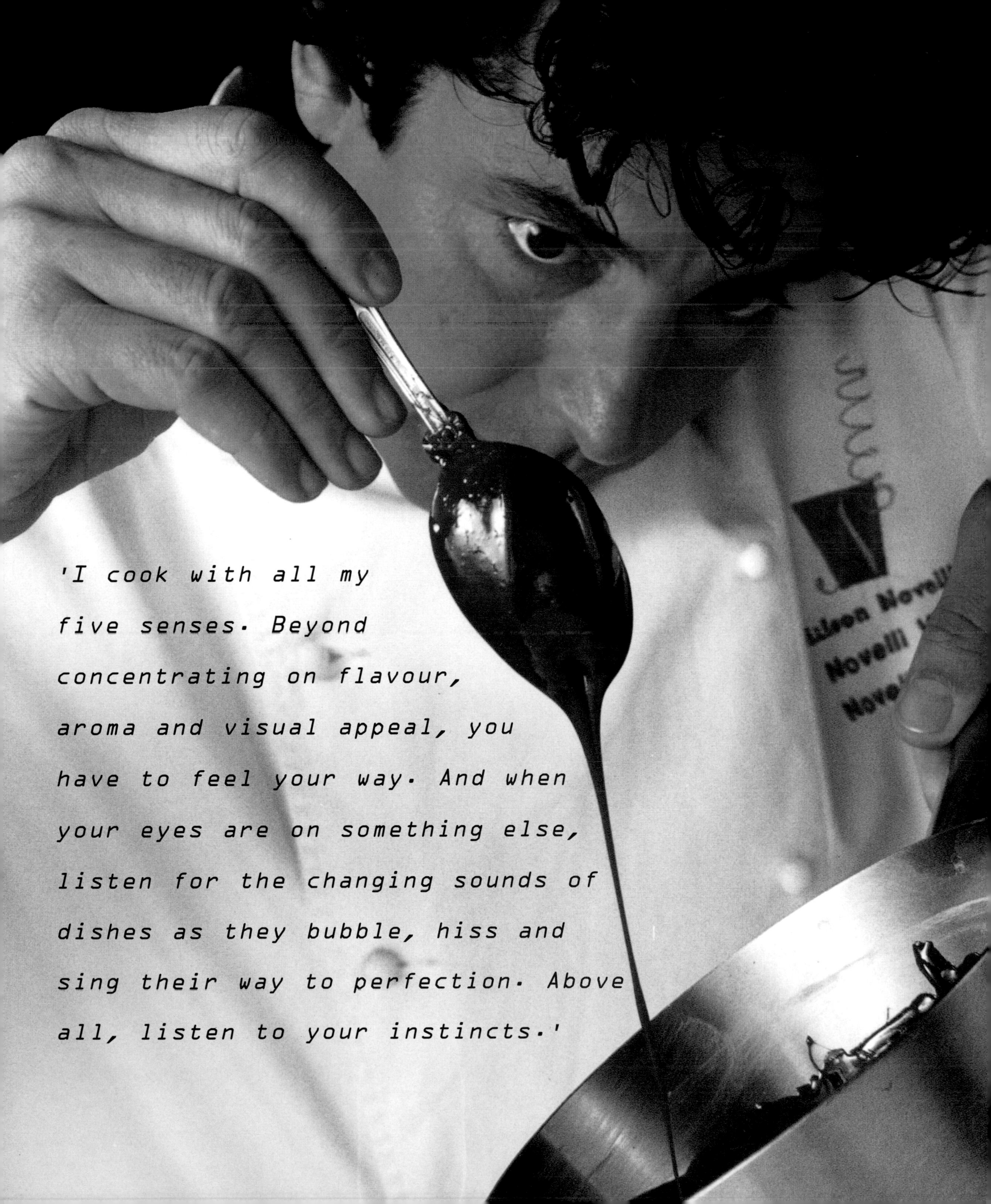

'I cook with all my
five senses. Beyond
concentrating on flavour,
aroma and visual appeal, you
have to feel your way. And when
your eyes are on something else,
listen for the changing sounds of
dishes as they bubble, hiss and
sing their way to perfection. Above
all, listen to your instincts.'

fish &

shellfish

When I see the fresh fish
arriving in the kitchens each morning
I find myself imagining the parts of the world
it has come from. I can smell the sea on the
scales, and I feel the creativity starting to
flow. I get so much pleasure from cooking fish,
because it is so easy to create a special meal
by doing very little. I hate to see wonderful
fish played about with or smothered in rich
sauces. Freshness is always the key. Look for
bright, shiny fish with clear eyes and pink
gills, but also remember that a really fresh
fish has no smell, until you begin to cook
it. All you should smell is the sea. If a
fish is old, then it smells fishy and it
is only fit for the bin. If a fish is
really fresh, you can even hear the crack
of freshness when you lift the gills,
like the stalk of a fresh flower
snapping. There are so many ways to
cook fish: all you need is the
confidence not to overcook it and
to let it speak for itself.

scallops

There is something very secretive and sensual about the scallop, a pearl of sweetness hiding inside a closed shell. It has an air of luxury about it, yet of all the crustaceans it is probably the best value for money. It looks delicate, but has the flavour and texture to combine with a surprising number of ingredients. Sometimes I worry that one day there won't be enough scallops left in the sea to feed our insatiable demand for them, because I can't imagine cooking without them.

Always buy hand-dived scallops, rather than dredged ones, which will have been dragged out of the sea at low-tide, picking up grit as they go. This can give them a grey colour, unlike the fresh white firm flesh of the hand-dived scallop. Unless your fishmonger can assure you that they have been hand-dived, it is best to choose scallops still in their shells. The shell of a dredged scallop will be broken up around the edges where it has been dragged. Hand-dived shells will be intact, and normally still covered in barnacles. Also, beware of the practice of soaking scallops to plump them up. As soon as you cook them, this liquid will ooze out and the scallops will shrink.

The shells should always be closed, or will close if you tap them. If the shell stays open, the scallop is dead. Hand-dived scallops are sorted and graded according to size by the divers. Buy the biggest you can (up to about 7 cm) for pan-frying, because they are the sweetest. The smallest queen scallops require only the shortest cooking. I like to drop them briefly into a flavourful nage (a court-bouillon with cream, see the recipe on page 26), and serve them as canapés. Scallop corals (ie the roe) should be bright orange, plump and firm, not pale yellow and flat. The colour is usually another sign of freshness. When we pan-fry scallops we remove their corals, as they have quite a strong flavour which can dominate a dish. However, we often use them in sauces, to infuse their intense, fishy taste, or dry them and grind them to a powder for dusting fish.

If you haven't cut scallops from their shells before I suggest you ask your fishmonger to do it, as you might damage the flesh — and your fingers!

Pan-fried Scallops with Orange, Vanilla and Cardamom

The perfect pan-fried scallop has a golden brown, slightly caramelized crust and a centre that is just translucent. If the flesh is white and opaque all the way through, it will be dry and chewy.

To achieve that fabulous crust (and this applies to all fish and shellfish) it is important to get a well-proved or non-stick pan hot first, before you even add the oil, then get the oil very hot before you put in the scallops. If you add oil to a cold pan, you won't get the intensity of heat and the moisture will leach out of the scallop into the oil, boiling – rather than searing – the flesh, and causing it to toughen up. The idea is to seal that moisture inside the scallop as quickly as possible: cooking for no more than a minute on each side.

This recipe demonstrates perfectly the way that scallops work with unusual flavours to create something special, yet very simple to prepare. In this case the combination of orange, vanilla and cardamom perfectly complements the caramelized sweetness of the scallops.

serves 4

a little olive oil

freshly ground salt and black pepper

12 large scallops

100 g baby spinach leaves

200 ml Orange, Vanilla and Cardamom Infused
    Oil (page 11)

sprigs of sage, to garnish

1 Heat a frying pan until very hot, then add a thin film of olive oil. When this is also very hot, season the scallops and pan-fry them for 1 minute on each side, until golden brown.

2 Arrange the spinach on 4 serving plates. Place the scallops on top. The heat from them will wilt the spinach.

3 Drizzle some of the infused oil around each plate and garnish with the sage.

Glazed Scallops, Broad Beans, Orange, Vanilla and Cardamom

From the simple idea of pan-fried scallops flavoured with orange, vanilla and cardamom, you can build up a more elaborate dish using the intense reduction of those flavours, rather than the oil, to add a 'glaze' to the scallops, together with some broad beans and diced tomatoes. For the garnish you can make a feature of the vanilla pods.

serves 4

200 g broad beans
2 tomatoes
a little olive oil
freshly ground salt and pepper
8 large scallops
2 vanilla pods, split lengthwise
sprig of mint, chopped
Orange and Cardamom Reduction (page 11),
   seeds from ½ vanilla pod added while still
   warm

for the garnish:
4 large sprigs of chervil
1 punnet of mustard and cress

1 Blanch the beans briefly in boiling water, refresh under cold running water and pop the bright green beans out of their skins.
2 Blanch the tomatoes briefly in boiling water, pop them into a bowl of cold water, then remove the skins. Quarter the tomatoes, scrape out the seeds and dice the flesh into ½-cm cubes.
3 Heat a pan until very hot, then add a little olive oil and heat until this is also very hot. Season the scallops and then sauté them for 1 minute on each side, until golden brown. A few seconds before you take them from the heat, toss in the broad beans, vanilla pods, tomatoes and mint and season again.
4 To serve, arrange some broad beans and tomatoes in the centre of each plate, with 2 scallops on top and a halved vanilla pod tilting upwards between them. Drizzle over some orange and cardamom reduction and garnish with chervil and mustard and cress.

Scallop Feuillantine

Once you feel comfortable pan-frying scallops, you can build up a more complicated dish like this favourite of mine, which I created at The Four Seasons, and revamped for Les Saveurs.

serves 4

8 baby fennel bulbs

2 tomatoes

2 large sheets of filo pastry

2 egg yolks, beaten

olive oil, for sautéing

freshly ground salt and pepper

12 large scallops, corals reserved for sauce
   (see below)

1 lemon grass stalk, cut in 4 lengthwise

handful of chopped chives

chervil sprigs, to garnish

for the sauce:

a little olive oil

4 shallots, finely chopped

4 mushrooms, finely chopped

50 g bulb fennel, finely chopped

1 garlic clove, finely chopped

12 clean scallop corals (see above)

1 lemon grass stalk

500 ml white wine

500 ml fish stock

150 ml double cream

1 Preheat the oven to 180°C/350°F/gas 4.

2 First, make the sauce: heat a little olive oil in a heavy-based pan, add the chopped vegetables and garlic and sweat very gently, until the vegetables are translucent.

3 Heat a little more oil in another pan and sauté the scallop corals with the lemon grass for about 2–3 minutes. Add to the vegetables and garlic.

4 Pour in the wine and reduce by about one-third, then add the stock and reduce again by two-thirds. Add the cream, season and bring to the boil. Turn down the heat and simmer for 5 minutes. Sieve into a clean pan.

5 Meanwhile, blanch the baby fennel for about 1 minute in boiling salted water. Drain, refresh under cold running water and reserve.

6 Blanch the tomatoes briefly in boiling water, pop them into a bowl of cold water, then remove the skin. Quarter the tomatoes, scrape out the seeds and dice the flesh into ½-cm cubes. Reserve.

7 Lay out one sheet of filo pastry on a clean work surface and brush with the beaten egg.

Place the next sheet of filo on top and brush with egg again.

8 Leave the filo to dry for 3 minutes, then cut out eight circles, about 7 cm in diameter.

9 Place these circles, egg-glazed side down, on a baking tray lined with baking parchment. Cover with a sheet of baking parchment to prevent the pastry from rising, then bake in the oven for 3-4 minutes until golden.

10 Heat a frying pan until very hot, then add a little olive oil and heat until this is also very hot. Season the scallops and sauté them with the lemon grass for 1 minute on each side, until golden brown. As you turn them, put in the blanched fennel to heat through.

11 In a separate pan, heat a little olive oil, add the chopped tomato and chives and heat these through. Warm the sauce through.

12 Place a scallop in the centre of each plate, top with a baby fennel and a disc of filo. Follow this with 2 scallops, a strip of lemon grass, another baby fennel and the second disc of filo. Pour the sauce around, garnish with tomato mixed with chives and chervil.

'I can't conceive of my kitchen without scallops'

Queen Scallops with Artichoke Nage

In this recipe, the time is spent on preparing the nage, and the scallops are added literally at the last moment. Served in scallop shells, they make wonderful canapés or starters.

serves 4

4 artichokes

equal parts white wine and water, for
cooking

4 shallots, finely chopped

4 baby carrots, finely chopped

8 asparagus spears

48 queen scallops, plus 4 large or 12 small
shells for presentation

for the nage:

a little olive oil

4 shallots, finely chopped

1 garlic clove, finely chopped

1 celery stalk, finely chopped

6 mushrooms, finely chopped

1 bay leaf

sprig of thyme

200 ml white wine

100 ml fish stock

100 ml double cream

freshly ground salt and pepper

small bunch of chives, chopped

8 basil leaves, chopped

for the garnish:

mustard and cress

basil leaves

a little caviar or lumpfish roe

1 Prepare the artichokes: remove the stalks and peel away all the outside leaves. Remove the chokes (the hairy cores), to leave the white hearts.

2 Simmer in the white wine and water (enough to cover) for about 40 minutes, until tender. Drain, cut into wedges about the same size as the scallops and reserve.

3 Prepare the rest of the vegetables: blanch the shallots and carrots in boiling water for 1 minute, drain and refresh under cold running water. Reserve.

4 Peel and blanch the asparagus in the same way. Cut off the tips and halve lengthwise. Slice the stalk thinly. Reserve.

5 Make the nage: heat a little olive oil in a pan and sweat the shallots, garlic, celery and mushrooms with the herbs until soft but not coloured.

6 Add the white wine and simmer gently for about 30 minutes.

7 Add the fish stock and simmer for a further 20 minutes.

8 Add the cream and bring back to a simmer, season to taste, then take off the heat and put through a fine sieve.

9 Return the nage to the heat and add the reserved artichokes, shallots, carrots and asparagus. Bring to the boil, then add the scallops and immediately take the pan from the heat. Leave for 1 minute for the scallops to continue cooking, then stir in the chopped chives and basil.

10 Spoon into the scallop shells, reserving about 4 tablespoons of the liquid. Froth up this liquid with a hand blender and spoon a little froth over each shell. Garnish with mustard and cress, basil and caviar or lumpfish roe.

brochettes

When we have parties for guests at the restaurants I like to serve brochettes of baby squid and langoustines interspersed with basil leaves and cherry tomatoes. The brochettes are also one of our best-loved starters. Instead of skewers made from wood or metal I use stalks of lemon grass, which release their perfume and flavour into the seafood as the brochettes cook. It is a simple idea, but people love it.

King Prawn and Lemon Grass Brochettes

These scaled-down king prawn brochettes give a flavour of the restaurant version which follows, but take very little time.

makes 12

12 peeled raw prawns
4 stalks of lemon grass
12 large basil leaves
12 cherry tomatoes

for the marinade:
olive oil to cover
10 basil leaves
10 sun-dried tomatoes, chopped

well ahead, ideally the day before:
1 Mix the marinade ingredients, add the prawns and leave to marinate in the fridge overnight or throughout the day if you are serving the dish for dinner.

when ready to cook:
2 Peel the outer leaves from the lemon grass, until the stalks are thin and pointed, then cut each one into three.
3 When ready to cook, preheat a hot grill or barbecue. Remove the prawns from the marinade and wrap each one in a basil leaf. Thread a wrapped prawn and a cherry tomato on each lemon grass 'skewer'.
4 Grill or barbecue the kebabs for about 1 minute on each side, basting with the marinade, until the prawns are cooked.

Squid and Langoustine Lemon Grass Brochettes

This more extravagant version can be served with salad leaves as a starter or even a light lunch.

serves 4

12 raw langoustines or king prawns
freshly ground salt and pepper
12 prepared baby squid
24 basil leaves
4 stalks of lemon grass
20 cherry tomatoes
thyme leaves

for the marinade and sauce:
200 ml olive oil
2 tsp Basil Oil (page 11)
600 ml Sun-dried Tomato Juice (page 12)

to serve:
100 g frisée leaves
4 bunches of wild rocket
Sherry Dressing (page 11)
sprigs of chervil and dill, to garnish

when ready to cook:

8 Unless you are pan-frying the brochettes, preheat a hot grill or barbecue.

9 Make the sauce: put the remaining sun-dried tomato juice in a pan and bubble up until reduced to a syrup.

10 Remove the brochettes and tomatoes from the marinade. Barbecue, grill or pan-fry over a high heat on all sides until golden brown, basting and sprinkling on the thyme just before the end of cooking. Also barbecue, grill or pan-fry the halved cherry tomatoes briefly.

11 Combine the frisée and rocket and toss in the sherry dressing.

12 To serve, arrange some dressed frisée and rocket leaves in the centre of each plate and place a brochette on top. Pour the sauce over and around the brochette, and garnish with the cherry tomato halves and some sprigs of chervil and dill.

well ahead, ideally the day before:

1 Peel the langoustines or king prawns, leaving the tail piece in place. Make an incision along the back and remove any dark veins of intestinal tract. Season.

2 Rinse the squid bodies and tentacles well, pat dry and season both.

3 Wrap the langoustines or prawns in basil leaves, then place inside the baby squid bodies, leaving the tails sticking out.

4 Peel the outer leaves from the stalks of lemon grass, until the stalks are thin and pointed.

5 Using the sticks of lemon grass as 'skewers', thread each one first through a cherry tomato, then through one of the filled baby squid body (crossways), then through a basil leaf and some squid tentacles, second filled baby squid body, another basil leaf and another set of squid tentacles. Repeat with a third filled squid, final basil leaf and set of squid tentacles. Finish with a second tomato. Repeat this with the remaining lemon grass skewers. Reserve the remaining cherry tomatoes.

6 Make the marinade, mix together the olive oil, basil oil and one-third of the sun-dried tomato juice. Halve the remaining cherry tomatoes and add to the marinade.

7 Season the brochettes, then leave to marinate in this mixture in the fridge overnight or throughout the day.

cooking en papillote

The point of cooking en papillote (i.e. in a parcel of baking parchment) is to steam the fish in its own juices, then to open up the paper parcel on your plate, releasing all the wonderful aromas. When you make your parcel, which will look a little like a Cornish pasty, don't fold it up too tightly. It should be a little slack, so that the parcel can puff up with steam without the paper splitting.

Papillote cooking is most suited to small fillets of fish, because larger pieces would take too long to cook. The first recipe is for a simple sea bream papillote, the second is a more impressive restaurant variation, using mussels and coconut.

Sea Bream en Papillote with Lemon Grass and Shallots

serves 4

4 sea bream fillets, each about 180–225g, scaled and pin bones removed
100 ml olive oil
freshly ground salt and pepper
6 shallots, thinly sliced
2 garlic cloves, chopped
4 stalks of lemon grass, thinly sliced
a little egg white

1 Preheat the oven to 250ºC/475ºF/gas 9. Coat the fish in olive oil and season.

2 Take 4 large squares of baking parchment about 30 x 30cm. In the centre of each sheet, arrange a bed of shallots, garlic and lemon grass and season. Place a fillet of fish on top.

3 Brush the edges of the paper with egg white and fold them over the top of the fish. Bring the edges together and pleat a series of folds to seal, so that you have a paper packet resembling a Cornish pasty. Repeat until you have four packets.

4 Sprinkle a little water over each packet, place on a baking tray and bake in the preheated oven for about 8 minutes, until the parcel puffs up and turns crisp and brown.

5 Put the parcels on plates and cut open with scissors at the table.

mussels

I really love mussels cooked en papillote, as overleaf, which is ironic as when I was very young I didn't like mussels at all. In the North of France, where I come from, moules-frites (mussels and chips) are the equivalent of the English fish and chips. Everywhere you see vans selling them to eat out of paper. We used to buy mussels instead of chocolate bars.

I always thought of mussels as the dish of the poor. We didn't have much money, like most of the families we knew, so we would have soup and bread, or pancakes, and often mussels. Then one day, when my mother gave me mussels, she said to me: 'This might be the dish of the poor, but the more you eat, the more you have on your plate,' meaning the pile of shells you accumulate - with artichokes it is similar. It seemed a very clever idea to me and I liked eating mussels after that.

I would spend hours walking on the beach, trying to find mussels clinging to the rocks. Fishing didn't interest me, but looking for mussels and crabs was like searching for treasure. Sometimes I used to take a little stove on my bicycle and cook my finds on the beach. The mussels I found were always small — then, of course, I realized it was because other people had been there before me and left the small ones behind, because the large plump ones taste the best.

I will let you into the secret of how we make our mussels bigger. It might sound a little crazy, but it is a tip I learned from the local people in France. First you clean the mussels, then put them in a bucket with enough water to cover and a couple of handfuls of oats. Mix everything around with your hands, then mix again every six hours or so, for two days. The mussels will eat the oats and grow bigger.

Remember, as long as they are closed, they are alive and can feed. Before cooking, if any of the shells open and won't close when tapped, throw them away.

Sometimes, for fun, we serve the following dish accompanied by a straw, so that you can drink the juices while you pick up the mussels in your fingers - the best way is to use one emptied mussel shell like a pair of tweezers to remove the rest. The mussels should all open in the steam of the papillote, just as they would if you were steaming them in a covered pan with wine and herbs for *moules marinières*.

When you put your papillotes on plates ready to serve, my tip is to shake each plate gently, to disperse the liquid through the shells inside the packets before opening, so that the mussels are nice and moist. Be sure to discard any mussels that haven't opened.

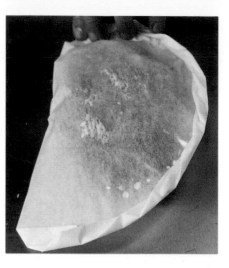

Mussel Papillote with Coconut Juice, Ginger and Lemon Balm

This is a dish to please all the senses. When you open up the papillote, the colour of the mussel shells and the aromas of coconut, ginger and lemon balm are fantastic.

serves 4

1.25 kg mussels

12 lemon balm leaves

50 g fresh ginger, finely chopped

2 stalks of lemon grass, sliced

juice and julienned zest of 1 lemon

juice and julienned zest of 1 lime

8 garlic cloves, thinly sliced

freshly ground salt and pepper

200 ml coconut milk

a little egg white

1 Preheat the oven to 250°C/475°F/gas 9. Scrub off all dirt and beards from the mussels. Clean them in seven changes of water, lifting out the mussels each time. Discard any that remain open.

2 Combine the lemon balm leaves, ginger, lemon grass, lemon and lime juices and zest, and the garlic. Add the mussels, season and mix well..

3 Take a large length of baking parchment, then spoon a quarter of the mussel mixture into the centre. (You might find it easier to press the paper into a shallow bowl, then spoon in the mussels; this stops them from rolling around!) Drizzle over a quarter of the coconut milk. Brush the edges of the paper with egg white. Then, taking care not to rip the paper gather it up and seal the edges together. Then pleat a series of folds around the edge to form a packet. Transfer the packet to a baking tray, and repeat until you have 4 packets.

4 Sprinkle a little water over each packet and put in the oven for about 10 minutes. When the paper is brown the mussels should be ready.

5 Serve in the bags on plates, and remember not to eat any mussels that have failed to open.

trout tartare

For me this dish is one of the best examples of how you can take a simple idea and present it just as it is, or develop and embellish it until it becomes something special.

I first made the tartare at The Provence Restaurant in Lymington in Hampshire, where I got my first Michelin star. These were what I call my 'crazy days', when I spent every minute trying to come up with newer and more original shapes, colours, flavours and textures for my dishes. If you will forgive me sounding sexist, I created this dish with women in mind, because we had many women lunching at the restaurant. It seemed to me that it was the sort of thing they wanted: light, fresh and easy to eat.

From the simple tartare, a combination of salmon trout (brown trout from the sea, rather than the river), asparagus and cucumber bound by a piquant anchovy mayonnaise, I dressed it up with a pool of gazpacho sauce, based on the flavours of the Spanish soup, crowned with wafer-thin slices of crisp cucumber and topped with a lightly boiled quail's egg and a sprinkling of caviar, and it has become one of my signature dishes.

Once I had made it the first time, the nightmare was to teach my team in the kitchen to do it quickly during service. I must have been a horror to work with, forever creating these dishes, then expecting my chefs to recreate them for fifty people. Like running a marathon, you do it over and over again, getting the time down each time. The biggest job is the cucumber crown, as the cucumber has to be sliced at the last minute, so that it stays crisp. Now, any chef in my restaurants can put together the tartare in two-and-a-half minutes.

Incidentally, the word 'tartare' used simply to refer to a kind of mayonnaise for serving with fish or a dish of seasoned raw minced steak (something that I cannot understand anyone serving or wanting to eat). These days, by extension, it is used for any dish in which the fish is marinated, rather than cooked. Unlike raw meat, however, the fish is first cured in salt.

If you don't want to make gazpacho sauce or cucumber crowns, the tartare makes a simple and satisfying starter without any extra elaboration, apart from some good bread. (I love Poilane bread from the famous Paris bakery; every day there are queues outside the shop for the moist Poilane sourdough, which is also distributed to local restaurants and flown around the world to chefs such as myself.) It also makes excellent canapés, spread on thin bite-sized pieces of bread. Alternatively, you could do as I do in my brasseries and garnish it just with an arrangement of salad leaves perched on top of the tartare.

Simple Trout Tartare

serves 4

450 g skinless fillets of fresh salmon trout
about 115 g sea salt
8 asparagus spears, trimmed
½ good deep green cucumber, halved
    lengthwise and deseeded
freshly ground black pepper

for the marinade:
500 ml olive oil
juice of 1 lime
good handful of chopped mixed herbs,
    such as basil, tarragon, lemon balm
1 head of garlic, halved

for the Anchovy
Mayonnaise:
2 egg yolks
1 tbsp white wine vinegar
1 tsp grainy mustard
5 anchovy fillets in oil, drained and
    coarsely chopped
5 basil leaves, chopped
200 ml olive oil
1 tbsp hot water

to serve:
4 large sprigs of chervil
some good bread

the day before, put the
trout to marinate:
1 Cover the trout completely on both sides
with the sea salt. Chill for 1½ hours.
2 Rinse the salt from the trout, drain well, pat
dry and place in a bowl.

3 Mix together all the marinade ingredients in a separate jug or bowl and pour over the trout. Leave in the fridge overnight.

next day:

4 Cook the asparagus in boiling salted water until just tender, refresh in cold water and drain. Then cut it into 5-mm dice and reserve.

5 Chop the cucumber into pieces the same size as the asparagus.

6 Make the anchovy mayonnaise: put all the ingredients except the olive oil and hot water in a blender or food processor and whiz together. Add the olive oil, drop by drop, continuing to blend and gradually increasing the addition of the oil to a trickle, then add the hot water until you have a thick, smooth mayonnaise (it is important to add the oil slowly and steadily in this way, rather than all at once, otherwise you run the risk of the mixture curdling). Season with pepper to taste. Reserve.

just before serving, assemble the tartare:

7 Remove the trout from the marinade, cut it into cubes of a similar size to the asparagus and cucumber, and combine all three together in a bowl. Add the anchovy mayonnaise and season with pepper (the anchovies will probably make the mixture salty enough). Mix thoroughly.

8 To serve: either pile the mixture into shallow bowls or plates or, for a neater presentation, place a 6-cm diameter pastry cutter in the centre of each bowl or plate. Pack each ring with the trout and asparagus mixture, pressing down as you do so. Neaten off the top, then carefully slide off the pastry rings. Garnish each serving of tartare with a good sprig of chervil and serve with the bread.

Trout Tartare with Cucumber Crown, Quail's Egg, Caviar and Chilled Gazpacho Dressing

One of the things I love about serving the tartare in this more elaborate way is that it combines different textures and temperatures, which really wake up the taste buds. The contrast inside the tartare of the slight crunchiness of asparagus and the softness of the trout is echoed in the garnish of crisp cucumber and softly boiled quail's egg. Served to perfection, the gazpacho dressing should be chilled, the tartare slightly less chilled and the egg just warm – not hot, or it will cause the tartare to melt and collapse.

serves 4

Trout Tartare as above

for the Gazpacho Dressing:
1 garlic clove, chopped
400 g cherry tomatoes
1 tbsp white wine vinegar
½ tsp unrefined caster sugar
½ tsp salt

squeeze of lemon juice
100 ml olive oil

for the garnish:
4 quails' eggs
½ cucumber, chilled
mixed salad leaves and herbs
Sherry Dressing (page 11)
4 tsp caviar or lumpfish roe
4 sprigs of chervil

several hours ahead, make
the gazpacho dressing:

1 Blanch the tomatoes briefly in boiling water, pop them into a bowl of cold water, then remove the skin and seeds and chop coarsely.

2 Using the same technique as for the anchovy mayonnaise, whizz the tomato flesh and all the remaining ingredients except the olive oil in a blender. Then, with the motor still running, add the olive oil, drop by drop as before, increasing the addition of the oil to a trickle, until you have a smooth dressing. Put through a fine sieve. Leave the mixture in the fridge until well chilled (at least 3 hours).

a few minutes before
serving:

3 Boil the quails' eggs for about 1½-2 minutes, depending on their size, then remove from the pan and dip briefly into a bowl of iced water to halt the cooking process. As soon as the eggs are cool enough to handle, carefully peel off the shells.

4 Using the pastry rings as before, place a round of tartare in the centre of each of four soup plates.

5 Slice the chilled cucumber in half lengthwise and scoop out the soft centre. Slice each length very thinly into half-moon shapes, preferably using a mandoline slicer. Toss the mixed leaves and herbs in the sherry dressing.

6 Place the cucumber halves in an overlapping circle around the outside edge of the top of the tartare. Arrange a bunch of mixed leaves and herbs in the middle of that, then nestle a quail's egg in the centre (fattest end downwards), and garnish with a little caviar or lumpfish roe. Decorate with sprigs of chervil.

7 Spoon the chilled gazpacho dressing around the base of the tartare and serve immediately – before the weight of the egg causes the tartare to sag!

cured & smoked salmon

Most people I know love the delicate flavour and texture of good smoked salmon, whether it is served on its own or used in more ambitious dishes. Every few days we smoke around a dozen salmon in the restaurant kitchens, as I have always believed in making as much of our own produce as possible.

You can buy domestic versions of catering smokers; or you could build your own, just as you would a barbecue. I have worked in various country restaurants where I used to build my own smokers. I liked to start the smoking process early in the morning so that when guests arrived for lunch they could have a drink outside, with the wonderful aromas of the smoking salmon giving them an appetite. I built my smokers with a brick surround, tall enough to install a grill about half a metre from the fire. As with a barbecue, you need to let your fire die down to embers, then smother it with oak sawdust to suffocate the red glow. It is very important that when the fish goes on the grill there is no flame, only smoke, as you don't want the salmon to cook. The oak will give a mellow character to the salmon. The smoker must be covered for at least three hours, so that the smoke envelops the fish: the flavour gains in strength the longer it is smoked. The salmon then needs to be wrapped in cling-film to retain the smokiness. It can be eaten immediately, but if you let it get colder in the fridge, it is easier to slice.

Before smoking, the fish has to be cured and then marinated. If you are buying a whole salmon, don't choose one bigger than 4.5 kilos (when the head and bones are removed, you will be left with two fillets of about 1.5 kilos), otherwise the fillets will be too thick, making it difficult to cure them through to the centre. Leave the skin on, as this will make the fish easier to slice later.

When you are planning to cure fish it must be absolutely fresh. For me wild salmon is the best, because it has a beautiful natural colour and its firmer texture won't become flabby during the process. Firmness is another attribute that will help you to slice the salmon more easily. Always use rock or sea salt, rather than fine salt, because it will cure the fish without making it taste too salty.

The recipe overleaf is for a basic marinade. You can vary it by adding a little sesame or truffle oil, or even a syrup of lemon grass, in a ratio of about two-thirds syrup to one-third of olive oil, giving a subtly different flavour to the salmon. To make the lemon grass syrup, boil 300 ml water with 100 g sugar, until the sugar dissolves, then simmer 10 broken-up lemon grass stalks in the syrup for 30-60 minutes. Remove from the heat and mix with the olive oil while still warm. Leave until completely cold before use.

Up to the point of smoking the fish, the curing and marinating process is the same as you would use to make gravadlax. If you want to do that, instead of smoking the salmon, roll it in a mixture of chopped dill and crushed peppercorns, then leave to cure in the fridge for about 3-4 days. Serve sliced very thinly.

makes about 3 kg

2 kg rock salt

2 tbsp unrefined sugar

two 1.5-kg fillets of very fresh salmon

for the marinade:

olive oil

1 head of garlic, roughly chopped

mixture of torn basil leaves, sprigs of thyme
   and bay leaves

10 shallots, sliced

early on the day before:

1 Mix the salt and sugar. Place the fillets on a tray and completely cover both sides with this mixture. Cover with cling-film and leave in the fridge for about 4 hours.

2 Make the marinade: heat a little olive oil in a pan and sweat the garlic, herbs and shallots very, very gently until they are just soft, but not browned. Then add enough olive oil to cover, and heat gently to allow all the flavours to infuse. Cover and leave to cool, then chill until completely cold.

3 Rinse the salt off the fish and pat dry. Put the cured salmon, skin side up, into the marinade (make sure it fully covers the fish) then leave, covered, in the fridge for at least 24 hours.

next day:

4 Remove the salmon from the marinade and pat completely dry, ready to put into your smoker. (Do make sure there is no excess oil, as it may set alight if it drips on the ash and burn the fish.) Smoke according to the instructions that accompany your smoker, or to taste (see previous page).

5 Serve thinly sliced with lemon juice, accompanied by good bread.

Home-smoked Salmon Salad with Spicy Aubergine Salsa, Poached Quail's Egg and Anchovy Dressing

Having smoked our own salmon, one of the ways we use it is in this simple salad.

serves 4

8 slices of smoked salmon

4 quails' eggs

200 g mixed salad leaves

fresh mixed herbs, to garnish

for the Aubergine Salsa:

3 tbsp olive oil

salt and freshly ground black pepper

1 large aubergine, finely diced

6 shallots, finely chopped

2 tsp sherry vinegar

25 g ground cumin

6 cardamom seeds

1 tsp garam masala

2 large gherkins, finely diced

10 sprigs of coriander, chopped

10 basil leaves, chopped

small bunch of chives, chopped

for the Anchovy Dressing:

300 ml olive oil

125 g anchovy fillets in oil, drained

2 tbsp white wine vinegar

½ tsp chopped garlic

2 tsp water

freshly ground salt and pepper

1 Make the aubergine salsa: heat 2 tablespoons of the olive oil in a large pan, season the aubergine and cook it slowly with the shallots, until the oil has been absorbed and the aubergine is soft.

2 Add the vinegar, spices and gherkins. Pour into a bowl and add the chopped herbs and the remaining oil . Cover with cling-film and leave until cold for the flavours to infuse. Adjust the seasoning if necessary.

3 Make the anchovy dressing: put all the ingredients into a blender or food processor and whiz to mix. Season and reserve.

4 Poach the quails' eggs (see opposite).

5 To assemble: arrange the smoked salmon slices in the centre of four plates and spoon some aubergine salsa around them.
Toss the mixed salad leaves in the anchovy dressing, pile neatly in the centre of the salmon, top with a quail's egg and garnish with the mixed herbs.

poached quails' eggs

I like to use poached quails' and chickens' eggs as a garnish for salads. There is something delightful about the way a perfect soft warm poached egg breaks into cold crisp salad.

There is a saying in the restaurant trade that you can tell the calibre of a chef by the way he cooks eggs, and poaching is a very good test. This technique might sound a bit laborious, but I still think it is the best. In cooking, however, the simplest things are often the most difficult to achieve. You need to practise to find perfection.

In a busy restaurant kitchen we have to prepare poached eggs in advance of service, and it can make life easier at home, too, if you are preparing eggs for a number of guests. They can be kept in the fridge until you need them, when all you have to do is dip them in a pan of boiling water for 20 seconds — just long enough to heat the yolks without overcooking.

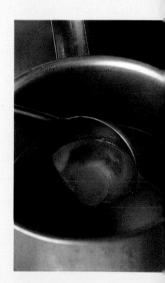

1 To a deep pan, add about one part white wine vinegar to nine parts water. (Vinegar helps to coagulate the white of the egg, but be careful not to add too much or it will give a sour taste to the egg.) Also don't salt the water, as the salt will counteract the effect of the vinegar.

2 Bring the water to a steady simmer.

3 Take a ladle and grease it with oil and the tiniest drop of white wine vinegar (this will begin to work on the egg white even before it goes into the water).

4 Break your egg carefully into the ladle. The chef's way to do this is to hold the egg in one hand, tap it very gently against a sharp edge, then separate your thumb and fingers, in order to pull apart the shell (when I worked part-time at the local bakery as a schoolboy, there were so many eggs to crack that I used to do them two at a time, one in each hand).

5 Lower the ladle slowly into the water, letting the water lap around it, so that the heat begins to set the white around the yolk. Don't let the water boil rapidly or it will disperse the white of the egg.

6 Let the ladle rest on the bottom of the pan briefly before turning the egg out. The egg will float upwards, sending up a parachute of white. At this point you can skim off any scum which rises to the surface, so that you can see what is happening more clearly. It should take about 1½-2 minutes for the white to firm up, leaving the yolk still soft (allow about 2-2½ for a chicken's egg).

7 Lift the eggs out carefully with a slotted spoon. If you want chickens' eggs to look their best, trim off any ragged edges of white with scissors. You really don't need to do this with quails' eggs as there is so little white. Transfer them into a bowl of iced water to stop them cooking any more.

Glazed Cured Salmon and Beaufort Cheese Terrine

This quite extravagant dish, which I created when I took over at Les Saveurs, is a way of using salmon which has been cured in salt and marinated as described on page 40, but not smoked — so it is a cousin of the marinated trout used for the tartare on page 35. Any substantial trimmings from the salmon left over from cutting it to fit the terrine could be used to make that dish, simply substituting the marinated salmon for the trout.

My inspiration for this dish came from the kind of combination of ingredients I like to see in a salad. A layer of pancetta surrounds the salmon, Ratte potatoes (small waxy salad potatoes), artichokes and cheese, which are combined with garlic, thyme, eggs and cream. When the terrine is sliced, pan-fried and glazed, it takes on a smoky character that goes very well with the intense sweetness of the balsamic vinegar reduction.

makes one terrine of around 12 portions

500 g Beaufort or Gruyère cheese, diced

1 litre dry Alsace or Riesling wine

1 fillet of salmon, about 1.5 kg, cured and
    marinated as described on pages 39–40

20 slices of pancetta

2 tbsp thyme leaves, picked and washed

4 garlic cloves, crushed

freshly ground salt and pepper

20 Ratte potatoes, boiled and sliced

12 large cooked artichoke hearts

500 ml double cream

3 whole eggs, plus 3 extra yolks

a little olive oil

for the Balsamic Reduction:

100 ml aged balsamic vinegar

3 tbsp Madeira

3 tbsp port

ideally two days before:

1 Put the cubed cheese into a bowl with the wine and leave to marinate overnight.

next day:

2 Preheat the oven to 150°C/300°F/gas 2.

3 Trim the marinated salmon along its length and ends to make a rectangle of the right length to fit into a large terrine.

4 Line the terrine with 3 layers of cling-film, leaving an overhang of about 20 cm over each side to wrap over the top once filled.

5 Line the cling-film with strips of pancetta, again leaving an overhang all round to pull over the top of the terrine when filled.

6 Remove the cheese from the marinade with a slotted spoon and use half of it to make a layer on top of the pancetta. Sprinkle with a little thyme and garlic, and season (do this for every layer).

7 Follow with a layer of half the potato slices.

8 Lay six of the artichoke hearts in a line down the centre.

9 Place the salmon fillet on top.

10 Continue the layers of cheese, potato and artichoke as before, sprinkling each layer with thyme, garlic and seasoning as you work.

11 Whisk the cream with the eggs and yolks until well combined. Season, then pour this mixture over the top.

12 Pull the overhanging layers of pancetta neatly over the top to completely enclose the terrine.

13 Pull the overhanging layers of cling-film over the top, tucking in the opposite side with a palette knife. Repeat all the way round.

14 Cook in a bain-marie in the oven for 1-1½ hours, until just set. Allow to cool.

15 Cut a piece of thick cardboard to fit the top of the terrine. Press down gently, then wrap the entire thing as tightly as possible in cling-film, place something heavy on top, and leave in the fridge for about 12 hours.

to serve:

16 Make the balsamic reduction: mix all the ingredients in a pan and simmer very slowly until reduced to a syrupy consistency.

17 Slice the terrine about 2 cm thick.

18 Heat a little olive oil in a large frying pan and pan-fry the slices briefly over a high heat, until golden and glazed on each side and heated through to the centre.

19 Unleash your artistic side with bold patterns of the balsamic reduction on the plates and place a slice of terrine on each.

Tuna Carpaccio

serves 4

about 115 g rock salt

500 g very fresh tuna loin, trimmed

for the marinade:

500 ml olive oil

handful of mixed rosemary, thyme and basil

1 garlic clove, lightly crushed

pinch of whole black peppercorns

juice of ½ lemon

to dress and garnish:

100 ml each light and dark soy sauce

a little vegetable oil

1 shallot, thinly sliced

1 thin slice of ginger, finely chopped

1 garlic clove, finely chopped

125 ml sesame oil

150 g beansprouts

a little chopped coriander and basil

4 sprigs of chervil

the day before:

1 Put the tuna on a plate and cover on both sides with rock salt. Chill for 2 hours.

2 Rinse the salt from the fish, pat dry and place in a bowl. Mix all the marinade ingredients and pour over the tuna. Chill overnight.

next day:

3 Remove the tuna from the marinade, pat dry and wrap tightly in cling-film. Chill for about 4 hours until firm.

4 To make the dressing, put the soy sauces in a pan and reduce by two-thirds. In a separate pan, heat a little vegetable oil and gently sweat the shallots, ginger and garlic until softened. Add to the soy sauce. Cool, then whisk in the sesame oil.

5 Cut the tuna into slices about 1 mm thick (about 20 slices).

6 Heat some more vegetable oil in a pan and stir-fry the beansprouts quickly to heat through. Add the chopped coriander and basil, season and stir in a little of the dressing.

7 Arrange the tuna slices with one in the centre of the plate and the rest overlapping around the outside. Season with pepper. Top with a spoonful of beansprouts and drizzle the rest of the dressing around. Garnish with chervil.

Mackerel Escabèche

In an *escabèche* the fish is marinated in oil, vinegar and herbs. Usually it is cooked first, but in this dish we marinate, *then* roast the mackerel.

serves 4

4 mackerel fillets, all bones removed

handful of chopped coriander

for the escabèche:

1 tsp coriander seeds

4 cardamom pods

4 shallots, thinly sliced

3 carrots, thinly sliced

1 red and 1 yellow pepper, peeled, deseeded and thinly sliced

1 baby fennel bulb, thinly sliced

1 tsp fine julienne of lemon zest

1 tsp fine julienne of orange zest, plus the juice of ½ orange

3 tbsp white wine vinegar

3 tbsp olive oil

1 tsp chopped coriander

pinch of saffron

for the garnish:

Dried Carrot Slices (page 15)

a few sprigs of chervil

the day before:

1 First, make the escabèche: crush the coriander seeds and cardamom pods lightly with a rolling pin, then put these and the rest of the escabèche ingredients into a pan. Cover and cook gently for 5-10 minutes, until the vegetables are cooked and soft. Remove from the heat, transfer to a bowl and leave to cool.

2 Score the flesh of each mackerel fillet through the skin widthwise along its length, then roll up and secure with cocktail sticks. Put the fish into the escabèche mixture, cover, turn to coat and leave overnight, turning from time to time when you can.

next day:

3 Preheat the oven to 220°C/425°F/gas 7. Remove the fish from the escabèche mixture, reserving the mixture.

4 Heat an ovenproof frying pan. When it is hot, put in the fish and seal quickly on both sides.

5 Add 2 tablespoons of the escabèche liquid and the chopped coriander, then transfer to the oven for 4 minutes. Add the vegetables from the escabèche for the last minute.

6 To serve: make a little mound of the vegetables on each of 4 plates. Remove the cocktail sticks from the fish fillets and place them on top. Pour the remaining pan juices over the top. Garnish each plate with some carrot slices and chervil.

smoked haddock

The British love smoked haddock and I love it too. I was first introduced to the combination of smoked haddock and eggs when I had to take my turn preparing the breakfasts at Chewton Glen Country House Hotel. Later I began to think of ways of presenting these two ingredients on lunch and dinner menus.

The first recipe is a simple assembly with puff pastry and hollandaise sauce. If you want to be a bit more adventurous, you can make the haddock into a brandade, which can be served with good bread, or as a filling for a baked potato, topped with a poached egg. To take this idea a stage further, we serve the brandade inside a baby pumpkin. We always try to use produce that is as natural as possible. Undyed smoked haddock usually indicates a higher quality of fish than the garish, yellow-dyed variety.

Smoked Haddock with Poached Egg and Puff Pastry

When we make our hollandaise sauce, we use clarified butter, which helps to prevent separation.

serves 4

1 sheet of ready-made puff pastry

1 egg yolk, beaten

2 fillets of undyed smoked haddock, each about 200 g

300 ml milk

25 g butter

4 eggs

3 bunches of watercress, stalks removed

a little Sherry Dressing (page 11)

for the Hollandaise Sauce:

100 g butter, preferably clarified

2 egg yolks

1 tbsp white wine

1 tsp white wine vinegar

1 tbsp water

freshly ground salt and pepper

for the garnish:

mustard and cress

1 Preheat the oven to 220°C/425°F/gas 7.

2 Clarify the butter for the hollandaise sauce by heating it over a very low heat without stirring. Skim the foam from the surface, then remove the pan from the heat and leave to stand for a few minutes. The white milk solids will sink to the bottom, allowing you gently to pour off the yellow clarified butter from the top. Reserve this and discard the white solids.

3 Make the hollandaise sauce: place all the ingredients except the butter in a round-bottomed bowl and place over a pan of simmering water. Whisk in a figure-of-eight motion as fast as possible until the sauce becomes as thick as whipped cream, then remove from the heat and slowly whisk in the butter. If the sauce thickens too much, adjust it by whisking in a spoonful of hot water. Season to taste, and keep warm. Do not allow to boil or the sauce will separate.

4 Roll out the puff pastry to a thickness of about 3 mm and cut 4 shapes of your choice. With the tip of a knife, score the top in diamond shapes, brush with the egg yolk and bake in the preheated oven for about 5 minutes until

puffed up and golden. Reserve.

5 Use tweezers or small pliers to remove the pin bones from the haddock fillets and cut them to produce 4 equal portions.

6 Place the fish in a deep oven pan with the milk and butter and put in the preheated oven for approximately 8-10 minutes (or until the skin comes away easily).

7 Poach the eggs as described on page 41.

8 To assemble: halve each puff pastry shape across, to create a base and lid. Place a puff pastry base in the centre of each plate. Dress the watercress with sherry dressing and place a small mound on top of the puff pastry base. Strip the skin from the haddock and place a portion on top of the watercress. Top with a poached egg and spoon some hollandaise sauce over the top. Finish off with a lid of puff pastry and garnish with mustard and cress.

Smoked Haddock Brandade

If you like, you can bake two large potatoes in the oven, rather than boiling them.

Brandade is good with bread and salad, or some roasted peppers.

serves 4

3 large potatoes
1.5 kg fillets of undyed smoked haddock
2 garlic cloves, coarsely chopped
2 sprigs of thyme
about 600 ml milk
10 basil leaves, chopped
freshly ground salt and pepper

1 Cook the potatoes in boiling salted water until tender, drain and mash.

2 Poach the haddock with the garlic and thyme in enough milk to cover, until the fish is cooked and flakes away from the skin. Drain, reserving the milk.

3 Remove the skin from the haddock and mash the flesh with the garlic and thyme. Mix in the potato and basil. Season to taste (go easy on the salt, as the haddock may be quite salty). If the mixture is too dry, add a little of the reserved milk.

4 Serve with slices of good bread.

Steamed Pumpkin and Smoked Haddock Brandade with Poached Egg and Baby Vegetables

serves 4

4 baby pumpkins
assorted baby vegetables, such as sweetcorn,
    carrots, fennel, to serve
Smoked Haddock Brandade (see above)
4 eggs
a little butter

1 Steam the pumpkins until the skin is soft enough for the point of a knife to go through easily.

2 Meanwhile, cook the baby vegetables in boiling salted water until just tender, drain and reserve.

3 Slice the tops off the pumpkins, remove the seeds and scoop out the flesh. Mix the pumpkin flesh with the brandade and spoon back into the pumpkins.

4 Poach the eggs (see page 41) and place one on top of each brandade-filled pumpkin. Replace the pumpkin lids.

5 Heat a little butter in a pan and toss the baby vegetables in it to heat through, season and arrange around the pumpkin.

grilled sole

In the restaurants we tend to pan-fry, rather than grill, because this is easier to control in a busy kitchen situation. When you have the luxury of cooking at home, however, it is an excellent way to treat a slim fish, such as sole.

Always grill fish under a moderate heat on a grill pan that is about 8 cm from the heat source. Put it higher and the fish will burn, lower and the fish will boil in its own juices.

Grilled Lemon Sole on the Bone with Gem Lettuce and Ginger Sauce

This is one of the quick and simple dishes we serve in the brasseries.

serves 4

50 g broad beans
2 tomatoes
4 whole lemon sole
a little olive oil
4 shallots, finely chopped
1 tsp ground ginger
1 tsp fresh root ginger, finely chopped
100 ml white wine
150 g unsalted butter
freshly ground salt and pepper
1 Gem lettuce, thinly shredded
small bunch of chives, chopped
squeeze of lemon juice

for the garnish:
mixed herbs
mustard and cress

1 Preheat a moderate grill. Blanch the broad beans in boiling water for 1 minute, drain and refresh under cold water. Reserve.

2 Blanch the tomatoes briefly in boiling water, pop into a bowl of cold water, then remove the skin. Quarter the tomatoes, scrape out the seeds and dice the flesh into $1/2$-cm cubes. Reserve.

3 Grill the sole, skin side uppermost first, for about 3 minutes on each side.

4 Heat a little olive oil in a pan and sweat the shallots with the ground and fresh ginger until soft but not coloured.

5 Add the white wine and simmer until almost all the liquid has evaporated.

6 Remove the pan from the heat and whisk in the butter. Season.

7 Just before serving, add the beans, lettuce, tomatoes and chives. Squeeze in some lemon juice.

8 To serve: place a sole on each plate, pour the sauce over and around, and garnish with herbs and mustard and cress.

'These colours, these flavours, speak to me of the Mediterranean.'

Andalouse of Sole

This is a much more dramatic way to serve any type of sole.

serves 4

4 large sweet tomatoes on the vine

a little olive oil

2 garlic cloves, chopped

handful of chopped thyme

4 medium tomatoes

1 litre Sun-dried Tomato Juice
  (page 12)

4 large Dover sole fillets, halved

freshly ground salt and pepper

100 g Picholine or other black
  olives

4 chunks of Aubergine Caviar
  (page 116), made with 1 baby
  aubergine

10 basil leaves, chopped

1 tsp Red Pepper Reduction
  (page 12)

for the garnish:

8 slices of Dried Aubergine
  (page 15)

a little olive oil

more Red Pepper Reduction
  (page 12)

well ahead, ideally the day before:

1 Blanch the large tomatoes briefly in boiling water and drop into a bowl of cold water. Remove the skins, then cut in half across their middles, leaving the stalk on, and scoop out the seeds. Put on a baking tray, sprinkle with olive oil, half the garlic and the thyme, and leave in the oven at its lowest setting, until not quite dried but taking on the character of sun-dried tomatoes, 4-5 hours. Reserve.

about 20 minutes before serving:

2 Blanch and skin the rest of the tomatoes and cut into quarters, remove the seeds and dice the flesh into ¹/₂-cm cubes. Reserve.

3 Preheat a moderate grill. Reduce the sun-dried tomato juice to a syrup in a pan. Keep warm.

4 Brush the sole fillets with a little olive oil and season. Grill for about 2-3 minutes on each side, skin side upwards first. If quite thick, they may even need 4 minutes on each side.

5 Put the diced tomatoes, olives, aubergine caviar and remaining garlic in a pan with the basil, halved tomatoes and red pepper reduction to heat through. Season.

6 To serve: pick out the chunks of aubergine caviar and place one in the centre of each plate. Place the bottom half of a baked tomato on top and fill with the olive and tomato mixture. Criss-cross two halves of sole fillet on top. Follow with 2 slices of dried aubergine, brushing both tomato and aubergine with oil to give them a sheen. Place the top half of the tomato on top. Spoon some red pepper reduction around.

poached turbot

There is nothing more beautiful than a piece of poached turbot. If you fry or roast it, it becomes tough, whereas if you poach it, it stays tender and moist.

The secret of poaching is doing it very, very gently, with the bubbles barely breaking the surface of the liquid, so that the fish stays intact.

Turbot Poached in a Fragrant Nage

The nage may be used immediately or kept in a sealed container in the fridge for 2 or 3 days. Serve the turbot simply, with some puréed potatoes or vegetables.

serves 4

4 darnes (thick boneless slices) of turbot, each about 200 g

for the nage:

a little olive oil

4 shallots, coarsely chopped

4 small carrots, coarsely chopped

1 celery stalk, coarsely chopped

2 garlic cloves, chopped

5 lemon balm leaves

1 bay leaf

1 sprig of thyme

1 tbsp coriander seeds

1 tbsp white peppercorns

1 star anise

zest of 1 lemon

200 ml white wine

freshly ground salt and pepper

1 First make the nage: heat the oil in a large heavy-based pan and sweat the vegetables, herbs, spices and lemon zest in it gently until the vegetables are soft but not coloured.

2 Add 300 ml water and the wine. Season and simmer for 5 minutes. Then remove from the heat and leave to infuse for about 20 minutes.

3 Put the nage back on the heat and bring to a simmer. Put in the turbot and simmer for 8 minutes.

4 Remove from the heat and leave the fish to rest in the nage for 2 minutes. Remove it from the nage and keep warm.

5 Pass the nage through a fine sieve and reheat if necessary. Serve with the fish.

Poached Turbot with Spinach and Almond Cauliflower Purée and Coconut Sauce

I first made this dish at The Four Seasons, where we had a lot of Asian customers. Previously I used to do a velouté of turbot, then I tried the dish using coconut milk — and it worked perfectly. Turbot is a relatively bland fish which soaks up such flavours very well.

serves 4

4 darnes (thick boneless slices) of turbot, each about 200 g

for the poaching liquor:

1 large can of coconut milk, about 400 ml

juice of ¹/₂ lime

2 tbsp white wine

4 shallots, chopped

10 g fresh root ginger, chopped

10 g lemon grass, chopped

10 g coriander seeds, crushed

10 leaves of fresh coriander

3 lime leaves

freshly ground salt and pepper

for the Cauliflower Purée:

200 g waxy potatoes, peeled and coarsely chopped

200 g cauliflower, coarsely chopped

1 garlic clove, chopped

about 600 ml milk

freshly ground salt and pepper

25 g butter

1 drop of almond essence

for the garnish:

2 large tomatoes

a little olive oil

100 g baby spinach

handful of chopped chives

1 tbsp Carrot Powder (page 15)

mixed herbs

4 slices of Dried Lime (page 15)

1 First make the cauliflower purée: put the potato and cauliflower in a pan with the garlic and enough milk to cover. Season. Simmer until the vegetables are very soft to the touch, then drain off three-quarters of the milk.

2 Add the butter and almond essence and whiz in a blender until smooth. Season again to taste and keep warm.

3 Cook the fish: mix together all the ingredients for the poaching liquor and simmer the mixture, without allowing it to boil, for 10 minutes. Remove from the heat and leave for about 20 minutes to infuse.

4 Bring the liquor back to simmering point and put in the fish. Simmer for 8 minutes, then remove from the heat and leave to rest for 2 minutes in the liquor.

5 Remove the fish and keep warm. Put the liquor through a fine sieve into a pan and warm through.

6 Meanwhile, prepare the garnish: first make tomato concassé by blanching the tomatoes briefly in boiling water, then popping them into a bowl of cold water and removing the skin. Quarter, scrape out the seeds and cut the flesh into ¹/₂-cm dice.

7 Heat a little olive oil in a pan, toss in the tomato concassé and heat through. Season.

8 Place the baby spinach in a warm stainless steel bowl with a little olive oil and chopped chives. Season and stir with your hand to wilt the spinach.

9 Froth up the reserved poaching liquor with a hand blender.

10 To serve: pile a little spinach in the centre of each plate and spoon some cauliflower purée on top. Place a darne of turbot on top of the purée and decorate with the warm tomato concassé. Spoon the frothy sauce around the fish. Lightly dust with carrot powder and top with herbs and a slice of dried lime.

'This dish plays with Asian flavours and a classic concept. I add almond to the cauliflower purée, which complements the flavour of the coconut.'

roasted sea bass

When chefs talk about 'roasting' fish, what they mean is starting off the cooking process by searing it in a frying pan over a very high heat and then finishing it in the oven. For me this is the best way to cook thick fillets of fish such as sea bass. The idea is to get a golden crust on the outside, which will seal the soft, moist flesh inside. If you were to poach sea bass it would become rubbery.

You need a metal-handled, non-stick frying pan that will transfer to the oven. As when cooking scallops, get it good and hot before adding the oil, and then get the oil really hot before you put in the fish, so that it will seal straightaway. Always seal the fish on the skin side first, very briefly, then flip the fish over and seal briefly again. Transfer it to a hot oven (220°C/425°F/gas 7), skin side down, for about 6-8 minutes. Because the skin is in contact with the pan, it will crisp up and protect the flesh from the heat.

It is always difficult to be precise about how long to cook a piece of fish, because it depends on the size and thickness. You can test it by inserting a cocktail stick into the centre of the fish. It is ready when the cocktail stick comes straight out, without any pulling or sticking. The fish will carry on cooking for a little longer after it comes out of the oven and, by the time it is on the plate, it will be perfectly done. If you worry too much that the centre of the fish is not quite cooked and then put it back into the oven, by the time it arrives on the plate it will be overcooked.

Roast Sea Bass with Basil and Chorizo

I love chorizo and one day I had the idea to cook it in oil, then use this oil for pan-frying bass. As the skin of the bass crisped up I discovered that it takes on an unbelievable flavour. From here it was only a simple step to cooking the fish and chorizo together. Mixing fish and meat is something I love to do, when the ingredients marry together as well as these. You can serve the combination quite simply, or build on the flavours to make the elaborate version we serve in the restaurant (overleaf).

serves 4

a little olive oil

4 bay leaves

60 g chorizo sausage, thinly sliced

4 fillets of sea bass, each
    about 200 g

a few basil leaves

1 Preheat the oven to 220ºC/425ºF/gas 7.

2 Get a large ovenproof pan very hot on the hob, before adding a little olive oil. When that is hot, add the bay leaves and briefly pan-fry the chorizo and sea bass, the latter skin side down. Flip over and cook the other sides briefly.

3 Turn the fish over again, so that it is skin side down and transfer the pan to the oven for about 5 minutes, or until the skin is golden and the flesh just cooked.

4 Served garnished with basil leaves.

sage beignets

These little deep-fried sage leaf parcels stuffed with olive paste make an attractive and unusual garnish — particularly with fish dishes. To make 16 sage beignets: wash 32 sage leaves and pat dry. Make some olive paste by processing 4 tablespoons stoned black olives with 1 garlic clove and moistening the mixture with a little olive oil. Season. Spread half the sage leaves with the paste and top each one with an anchovy fillet. Press one of the other sage leaves on top to sandwich. Mix 1 tablespoon of baking powder with 1 tablespoon of cornflour and 2 tablespoons of plain flour, and add just enough cold water to make a batter with the consistency of single cream. Coat each pair of stuffed sage leaves in batter and deep-fry in hot vegetable oil for 30 seconds to 1 minute, until puffed up and golden. Drain well on kitchen paper.

'Sea bass and chorizo –
so sexy together.'

Roast Fillet of Sea Bass with Chorizo Oil, Aubergine Caviar, Basil and Fennel

Here, the addition of two of my favourite flavours — sun-dried tomato and aubergine — turns the sea bass and chorizo into something extra-special. You could also try substituting merguez or any other hot spicy sausage for the chorizo.

serves 4

1 litre Sun-dried Tomato Juice (page 12)

8 baby fennel bulbs

a little olive oil

4 bay leaves

4 fillets of sea bass, each about 200 g

Aubergine Caviar (page 116)

60 g chorizo sausage, sliced

40 g black olives, halved

freshly ground salt and pepper

60 g tomatoes, blanched, skinned, deseeded
   and diced (see page 24)

8 cherry tomatoes

1 sprig of basil, separated into leaves

15 g unsalted butter

for the garnish:

4 tbsp Chorizo Oil (page 11)

Deep-fried Basil Leaves (page 16)

4 Dried Tomato Slices (page 15)

1 Preheat the oven to 220°C/425°F/gas 7. Put the tomato juice in a pan and bubble until reduced to a syrup. Reserve.

2 Cook the fennel in boiling water for about 3 minutes until al dente. Drain and keep warm.

3 On the hob, get a large ovenproof pan very hot before adding a little olive oil. When that is very hot, add the bay leaves and fry the sea bass briefly, skin side down. Flip the fish over and cook briefly.

4 Add the aubergine caviar (discarding the skin), cooked fennel, chorizo and halved olives. Season. Turn the fish over again, so that the skin side is down and transfer to the oven for about 5 minutes or until the skin of the fish is golden and the flesh just cooked.

5 Just before serving, add the chopped and whole cherry tomatoes with the basil, and adjust the seasoning if necessary.

6 Heat the tomato syrup gently in a pan and stir in the butter. Season to taste.

7 To serve: arrange the chorizo, fennel, olives and chopped tomatoes in the centre of each plate. Place a fillet of sea bass on top, together with a fried bay leaf. Pour some tomato syrup around, sprinkle with chorizo oil and garnish with deep-fried basil leaves, cherry tomatoes and a dried tomato slice.

poult

Confit of
duck or rabbit, roast
pigeon, cassoulet, these are
flavours that excite me, and that I have
known since I was a child, but one of the reasons
I left France was that I knew it would be easier
for me to try something different with them, away
from the classical French system of cooking. For
me the idea of turning a cassoulet into a
marbled terrine or serving venison with
scallops in a spicy sauce is an adventure.

Of course, that doesn't mean you can't
enjoy a simply roasted quail or pigeon, but
you could also roast some more quail to
make an elegant quail ravioli for later,
or serve your pigeon with a tarte
tatin of red onion.

It saddens me that so many people
have a game bird or a piece of venison
languishing in their freezer because
they simply don't know what to do
with it. I hope this chapter will
give some ideas.

quail & chicken

Unlike chicken, which are more forgiving, quail are precious little birds which you must be careful not to overcook. The very best way of cooking them is to spit-roast them, so they brown evenly all round. Of course, you can also seal them all over in oil in a pan, then transfer the birds to the oven, as in the recipe opposite. It could also be used for poussin, or for chicken — though you would need to increase the roasting time to 12 minutes for a poussin, or 30 minutes per kilo, plus 15 minutes, for a chicken.

Roast Quail with Grilled Pancetta

Instead of grilling the pancetta separately, which we do purely for garnish, you could use a little more and wrap it around the quail before cooking.

serves 4

olive oil

freshly ground salt and pepper

4 oven-ready quail

4 garlic cloves, unpeeled

4 sprigs of sarriette (summer savory)

4 bay leaves

12 peeled grapes

12 thin slices of pancetta

1 Preheat the oven to 200°C/400°F/gas 6.

2 Heat a little olive oil in a large ovenproof pan. Season the quail and brown them all over in the oil.

3 Crush the garlic cloves gently to release their flavour, then add them to the pan with the sarriette and bay, and roast in the oven for about 6–8 minutes, until the juices run clear when the thickest parts of the birds' thighs are pierced.

4 Just before the end of cooking time, add the grapes to the pan and heat through.

5 Grill the pancetta until crispy.

6 To serve: put the quail in warmed serving dishes. Cross 2 slices of pancetta on top of each quail and garnish with roasted sarriette and bay from the pan. Spoon the pan juices around.

Ravioli of Seared Quail and Foie Gras with Baby Leeks

Simply roasted quail is delicious as it is, but you can transform it into something more eye-catching by removing the breasts and legs and wrapping the breasts in fresh pasta to make a raviolo. This was just one element of the elaborate game plate I used to serve at The Four Seasons, which also included Pigeon Tarte Tatin, Rabbit Cutlets and Venison with Truffle Mousse. However, it makes a great starter just on its own.

serves 4

4 roast quail (as above), herbs and pan juices
   reserved
4 sheets of fresh pasta
8 large basil leaves
freshly ground salt and pepper
225 g preserved foie gras, sliced into four
   pieces
1 egg, beaten
100 ml veal or chicken jus
a little olive oil

for the leeks:

1 tbsp chicken stock
15 g butter
2 tbsp double cream
12 baby leeks

for the garnish:

4 tomatoes, skinned, deseeded and diced
   (see page 24)
a few chive stalks, finely snipped
chervil sprigs

1 Carefully remove the breasts and legs from the quail
and leave to cool.

2 Place the pasta on a floured board and from each
sheet cut one circle about 11 cm in diameter and one
approximately 7 cm in diameter.

3 Place a basil leaf in the centre of each of the larger pasta
circles. Lay a quail breast on top and season. Follow this
with a slice of foie gras, season again, then top with the
second quail breast. Finish with another basil leaf.

4 Place one of the smaller circles of pasta on top, brush the
edges of each pasta circle with a little beaten egg then
pinch the two together to completely enclose the quail and
foie gras. The ravioli will resemble pork pies in shape.

5 Cook the leeks: put the chicken stock, butter and cream
in a pan and bring to a simmer. Add the leeks and simmer
for about 4 minutes, until the sauce has thickened and
coated the leeks, which should be tender. Keep warm.

6 Make the sauce: bubble up the pan juices from cooking
the quail, add the jus and bring back to a simmer. Continue
to bubble until thickened to a sauce-like consistency, then
put through a fine sieve and season to taste. Add the quail
legs and keep warm.

7 Cook the ravioli: bring a large pan of salted water to the
boil, add a drop of olive oil and then put in the ravioli.
Simmer for 3 minutes, then remove with a slotted spoon.

8 Serve the ravioli on a bed of leeks, drizzle around the
sauce and garnish with the quail legs, crossed, diced tomato
and some chives and chervil.

By boning and stuffing chicken legs you can make something exciting from the parts of the chicken that are often thought of as the least interesting. Although, of course, the legs have a stronger flavour than the breasts, I find chicken a very bland meat, which marries well with quite rich combinations of flavours. I like to use a black pudding stuffing, similar to the one I use to stuff pigs' trotters.

I learned how to make black pudding when I was very young and working in a Martinique restaurant. Unfortunately the first time I made the puddings, the chef left me in charge, without properly explaining how to cook them. Instead of poaching them very slowly, I set them boiling and they exploded — about 200 black puddings all over the kitchen! I don't make them any more because there are now very strict regulations about their production, but I still love the richness they add to certain dishes. One of my favourite starters in the brasseries is a simple salad made with dressed leaves, black pudding and softly poached eggs.

Sometimes, for a change, we might stuff the chicken legs with a mushroom risotto or pipérade risotto (see page 125). You can use the same stuffings and method for rabbit legs.

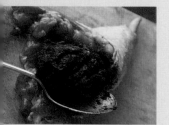

1 With a sharp knife cut off the foot end of the drumstick, then push the flesh back with your fingers a little, so that the bone protrudes.

2 To remove the thigh bone, first make an incision along the length of the top of the thigh, cutting right through to the bone.

3 Pull the flesh back, away from the bone, exposing it. Slide a knife underneath the bone to free it further from the flesh.

4 Cut through the joint between the thigh and the drumstick, then snap off the thigh bone and discard it.

5 Open out the flesh of the thigh, so that it lies flat on your work surface.

6 Season ready for stuffing.

7 Place some stuffing on the area where the thighbone has been removed.

8 Fold over the sides to enclose the stuffing.

9 Take a trussing needle and a length of butcher's twine, knot one end of the string and oversew the seam

(as though lacing up a boot with a single lace) to seal in the stuffing completely.

You can cook the stuffed chicken legs in any of the following ways):

*To roast, preheat the oven to 220°C/425°F/gas 7. Heat a little olive oil in a large ovenproof pan. Season the chicken legs and brown them all over in the oil. Transfer the pan to the oven and roast for about 10-15 minutes, until the juices run clear when the thickest part of the flesh is pierced.

*To confit the stuffed legs, follow the method described on page 74.

*To steam, season and wrap tightly in cling-film. Steam for 15 minutes, until the juices run clear when the thickest part of the flesh is pierced.

When the chicken is cooked, by whatever method, remove the string by pulling on the knotted end.

Spit-roast Chicken Leg Stuffed with Ox-cheek and Black Pudding, with Millefeuille of Apple

serves 4

4 chicken legs

4 sprigs of thyme

4 bay leaves

100 ml chicken jus, warmed

12 Dried Apple Slices (page 15)

for the stuffing:

250 g skinless chicken breast

freshly ground salt and pepper

1 egg

500 ml double cream

$^1/_2$ recipe quantity Beef Daube (page 97)

a little olive oil

150 g black pudding, skinned and chopped

1 garlic clove, chopped

4 shallots, finely chopped

10 basil leaves

handful of thyme leaves

for the Caramelized Apple:

25 g butter

2 Granny Smith apples, peeled and thinly sliced

1 tbsp icing sugar

1 tsp Calvados

1 Preheat the oven to 220°C/425°F/gas 7.

2 Bone the chicken legs as described opposite.

3 To make the stuffing, first make a chicken mousse: trim the chicken of all fat. Season and chop. Put into a food processor and blend to a paste. Add the egg and blend again for 10 seconds. Scrape the mixture down the sides of the bowl with a spatula. Add the cream very slowly, turning the machine off every few seconds to scrape down again, until everything is well incorporated. Put through a fine sieve.

4 Break down the beef daube into shreds. Heat a little olive oil in a pan and sauté the daube, together with the black pudding, garlic, shallots, basil and thyme. Season well and allow to cool, then mix in the chicken mousse.

5 Stuff the chicken legs with the mixture, sew up and roast with the thyme and bay leaves, as opposite.

6 Meanwhile, make the Caramelized Apple: melt the butter in a pan and add the apple and sugar. Cook over a moderate heat, until the apple is golden and just soft. Add the Calvados and stir over the heat to deglaze the pan.

7 Remove the chicken from the oven and undo the string by pulling on the knotted end. Slice across at an angle. Spoon some of the warm jus on the plates and arrange the chicken on top. Alongside, make a millefeuille by layering up the caramelized apple and dried apple slices. Garnish with the roast thyme and bay leaves.

pigeon

For me the best pigeons are the farmed ones that come from Bresse. They have a waxy, yellow-gold flesh that takes its colour from the maize on which the pigeons are fed and quite a thick skin, similar to a corn-fed chicken. Their flavour is rich, but not gamey.

Normally for roasting you would choose squab pigeons, which are the young tender ones, but Bresse pigeons are often bred to be quite large too, with a good amount of still tender meat on them, including the legs, so you can create a more substantial dish with them.

Wild or wood pigeon on the other hand have a darker, stronger-flavoured flesh, the breast meat of which lends itself well to marinating, and can be wonderful. However, wild pigeons have legs like Carl Lewis from running around all day, so they can be quite muscular and tough. The legs are best added to game casseroles and slowly cooked in red wine, or chopped up and used to make a rich sauce.

Like most game birds, whole Bresse pigeon or wild pigeon breasts need to be cooked only briefly or the flesh will dry and tighten up. As with most roasts and all but the smallest of game birds, the pigeon needs to be left in a warm place to rest for a few minutes after cooking to allow it to recover its juices.

Roast Pigeon with Red Onion Tarte Tatin

I like to serve roast pigeon with a tarte tatin made not with fruit, but with red or sweet white onion, simmered first in milk to draw out the acidity, then cooked in red wine, the deeper the flavour and colour the better. We add a dash of grenadine or port a few minutes before the end of cooking time to accentuate the dark colour, then glaze the tarts with honey, rather than caramel.

You could make the onion tatin as an unusual accompaniment to any simply roasted meat; alternatively, when you want to make something more impressive, use it as a base for the carved breasts and legs of a roasted pigeon layered up with baby vegetables as we do in the restaurants.

serves 4

a little olive oil

4 oven-ready pigeons

4 sprigs of thyme

4 sprigs of rosemary

4 bay leaves

4 garlic cloves, lightly crushed

4 individual Red Onion Tartes Tatins (see overleaf)

about 16 baby leeks, to garnish

for the Red Wine Sauce:

a little olive oil

6 shallots, finely chopped

1 celery stalk, finely chopped

2 garlic cloves, chopped

1 sprig of thyme, chopped

2 fresh bay leaves

6 black peppercorns

4 mushrooms, finely chopped

250 ml chicken jus

reserved red wine reduction from cooking the onions (see overleaf)

freshly ground salt and pepper

knob of butter

1 Preheat the oven to 220°C/425°F/gas 7. Prepare the red onion tartes tatins as described overleaf and put them into the oven with the pigeons (see below).

2 Heat a little olive oil in a large pan (or two smaller ones). Fry the pigeons gently, turning from time to time, until golden brown on all surfaces (make sure the legs, especially, are browned as this meat will take longest to cook).

3 Transfer the pigeons to a roasting pan, balanced on one leg, with a sprig of thyme and rosemary, a bay leaf and a crushed garlic clove laid over each. Roast for 5 minutes, then turn on the other legs and roast for 5 more minutes. Turn the birds on their breasts and roast for a final 5 minutes, until medium-rare (roast for a little longer if you prefer them more well done). Allow them to rest in a warm place 5–10 minutes after they come out of the oven.

4 Meanwhile, make the sauce: heat a little olive oil in a pan, add the shallots, celery, garlic, herbs and peppercorns, and soften without browning. Add the mushrooms and the chicken jus and bubble up until it is reduced by half and coats the back of a spoon. Add the red wine reduction saved from cooking the red onions for the tartes tatins and bubble up again until reduced to the consistency of double cream. Season to taste, then wave in the butter with a spoon to add shine to the sauce. Strain through a sieve into a clean pan and keep warm.

5 Prepare the garnish: blanch the baby leeks for about a minute in boiling salted water, refresh in cold water, and drain well. Heat a little olive oil in a pan and toss the blanched baby leeks to heat them through. Season.

6 Remove the tatins from the oven and, with a spatula, carefully flip them over, onion side up, on 4 plates. Be careful not to touch the hot caramel.

7 Serve the pigeon cut in half lengthwise alongside the tarte tatin and garnish each plate with a bundle of blanched baby leeks (use one leek to tie the rest in bundles).

red onion tarte tatin

Although we often do use red onions to make this dish — being mild, they suit the treatment — we more generally choose Saint-André onions from France, which are white. By the end of cooking, however, they have taken on a rich burgundy colour. By all means use red onions, but if you can get hold of Saint-André onions you will find that they are just that bit sweeter.

makes 4

225 g puff pastry (well chilled)

2 red onions or Saint-André or other sweet white onions (roughly the size of tennis balls)

300 ml milk

freshly ground salt and pepper

2 bay leaves

500 ml robust, deeply-coloured red wine

2 tbsp red wine vinegar

1 tsp chopped thyme

1 tsp chopped rosemary

dash of grenadine or port (optional)

4 tbsp clear honey

1 Preheat the oven to 220ºC/425ºF/gas 7.

2 Roll the pastry out to a thickness of about 3mm. Cut out 4 circles about 10 cm in diameter. Pile the pastry circles on a plate and keep in the fridge until required.

3 Peel the outside skin from the onions, but leave the base and stalk intact.

4 Pour the milk into a pan, season with salt and pepper, add the bay leaves and the onions and bring to the boil. Turn the heat down and simmer for about 10 minutes, until a knife inserted into an onion will go through the outside layers easily, but find the heart still crunchy. Drain in a colander.

5 Peel off the next outer layer of onion, and halve each one across the middle.

6 Pour the red wine into a pan, add the red wine vinegar and herbs and season with salt and pepper. Put in the onions cut side down. Bring to a simmer, then continue simmering for 10 minutes, adding the grenadine or port (if you are using them) after about 5 minutes (don't let the wine boil as you want to retain its fruitiness). As the wine reduces, roll the onions around from time to time, until they are well coated and almost tender in the centre.

7 If you like, strain what is left of the red wine reduction and reserve for a sauce.

8 Put the onion halves on a rack placed over the pan and leave until cold and dry. Trim off the roots and stalks.

9 Cover each onion half with a circle of pastry. Slightly tuck the edges underneath the edge of each onion.

10 In a shallow pan, heat the honey until it starts to bubble, then pour a little into each of 4 small tart tins. Place an onion half, in its pastry blanket, on top and cook in the preheated oven for about 10 minutes, until the pastry is golden brown and the edges caramelized.

11 Remove the tatins from the oven and, with a spatula, carefully flip them over, onion side up, on 4 plates. Be careful not to touch the hot caramel. Serve with the pigeon (pages 68–9) or any roast bird.

Roast Pigeon and Baby Vegetables Layered on Red Onion Tarte Tatin with Red Wine Sauce

This dish might look dramatic, but it is really just another way of serving the tarte tatin with roasted meat. When you trim the roots and stalks from the onions after they have been cooked in wine, take an extra slice away from the stalk end. This makes a good flat surface for laying the pigeon on top.

serves 4

4 individual **Red Onion Tartes Tatins** (see previous pages)

4 oven-ready pigeons

4 sprigs each of thyme and rosemary

4 bay leaves

4 garlic cloves, lightly crushed

16 baby carrots

16 baby leeks

16 baby turnips

16 silverskin onions

Red Wine Sauce (page 69)

4 chervil sprigs, to garnish

1 Make the tartes tatins as described on the previous pages, but take an extra slice off the base when trimming the cooked onions.

2 Cook the pigeon with the herbs and garlic as described on page 69.

3 While the tartes tatins and pigeon are in the oven, cook the carrots, leeks, turnips and silverskin onions in boiling salted water until just tender. Drain and reserve.

4 Start making the sauce as described on page 69 until reduced and coating the back of a spoon.

5 Remove the pigeon from the oven and carve off the breasts and legs. Keep them warm. Reserve the roasted herbs for garnish.

6 Put the pigeon bones and trimmings into the pan containing the sauce, then finish the sauce as described on page 69 and keep warm.

7 Remove the tatins from the oven and flip them over on 4 plates. Press each onion down gently if necessary to make a flat base for the pigeon.

8 Criss-cross the two pigeon legs on top, then arrange a few baby vegetables on top of them.

9 Next add the two pigeon breasts, leaning against each other, plus some more vegetables.

10 Pour a little sauce over the top, garnish with the reserved roasted herbs, silverskin onions and a sprig of chervil.

confit

You can't beat a well—made confit — duck or goose, or even pork, cooked very slowly with herbs in its own fat until the meat is meltingly tender. I also love rillettes, which are simply confit taken a stage further, so that the meat can be worked into a soft mixture. Since confit is such a classic dish, the inventiveness comes from finding new ways of presenting it.

Confit of Duck

serves 4

4 large duck legs, thigh bones removed (either ask your
    butcher to remove the bones or follow the method
    described on page 66)

about 250 g sea salt

2 onions, halved

2 carrots, halved

6 garlic cloves, lightly crushed

2 large sprigs of thyme

4 bay leaves

500 g duck or goose fat, melted

at least 6 hours ahead:

1 Trim all the excess skin and fat from the bottom of the thighs where the bone has been removed, to give the duck legs a shape similar to that of a chicken drumstick. Remove all the feather stubble from the skin. You can do this with a blow-torch, or hold the meat over a gas flame with a fork.

2 Put the duck legs into a shallow dish and cover with sea salt. Leave in the fridge for 3 hours to help the meat to tenderize.

3 Preheat the oven to about 150°C/300°F/gas 2. Remove the duck legs from the salt and rinse. Place in a pan with the onion, carrot, garlic, thyme and bay leaves. Cover with the duck or goose fat and leave in the oven for 2 hours, or until the meat almost falls off the bone. Leave to cool and set. Heat through to serve.

4 The confit can be stored in sealed containers in the fridge for up to a week until ready to use.

Potted Duck Rillettes with Gherkins

In the restaurant we serve rillettes with Poilane bread. You can keep the rillettes in the fridge for several days and you can also make rillettes with rabbit, if you prefer.

serves 4

4 large duck legs, prepared for confit as
   described opposite
10 shallots, very finely chopped
2 garlic cloves, crushed
1 bunch of chives, chopped
10 basil leaves, chopped
4 large gherkins, to serve
good bread, preferably sourdough, to serve

1 Confit the duck legs as described opposite, but leave them in the oven for about 2¹/₂ hours, until the meat falls completely from the bone.

2 Reserving the fat, remove the skin and bones from the duck.

3 While still warm, use two forks or your fingers to break the flesh down into a smooth soft mixture.

4 Put this in a bowl with the shallots, garlic, chives and basil. Mix together well.

5 Press into 1 large or 4 individual containers, such as ramekins, and spoon over some of the confit fat to create a protective film over the top.

6 Allow to cool and then store in the fridge until ready to serve.

7 Serve with the gherkins and bread.

Confit Duck Leg, Garlic Crust with Cassoulet Beans

This recipe features confit of duck leg baked with a garlic crust and served either with cassoulet beans or, as a variation, with black bean salsa, which we make by simmering presoaked black beans in chicken stock for about 1–1½ hours with some sweated herbs, garlic, onion, carrot and celery. When the beans are soft, they are finished with chopped gherkins, extra-virgin olive oil and some more fresh herbs.

serves 4

4 confit duck legs (as previous pages)
flat-leaved parsley, to garnish

for the Cassoulet Beans:
200 g dried white haricot beans
a little olive oil
100 g belly pork, chopped
1 onion, chopped
1 celery stalk, chopped
1 large carrot, chopped
4 garlic cloves, chopped
3 plum tomatoes, chopped
1 bouquet garni
500 ml chicken stock
a few leaves of basil, chopped

for the Garlic Crust:
2 slices of dry bread
4 garlic cloves, finely chopped or crushed
fresh thyme leaves, stalks removed

the day before:
1 Soak the haricot beans overnight.

Next day:
2 Heat a little olive oil in a large heavy-based pan, add the belly pork, vegetables, garlic, tomatoes and bouquet garni, and sweat gently until the vegetables are soft but not coloured.
3 Add the drained beans and cover with the stock. Simmer for about 1½-2 hours, until they are plumped up and soft. Stir in the basil.
4 Towards the end of the bean cooking time, make the garlic crust: whiz all the ingredients in a food processor until finely ground.
5 Preheat the oven to 200ºC/400ºF/gas 6. Remove the confit duck legs from their fat and roll in the crust mixture until well coated.
6 Cook the duck legs in the oven for about 6-8 minutes, until the crust is golden brown.
7 To serve: pile the beans on a plate, top with a duck leg and garnish with parsley.

cassoulet terrine

For this recipe I looked at the traditional dish of cassoulet, made with confit meats, sausage and haricot beans, took it apart and then reassembled the elements of the dish in a totally different way. I wanted to make a very visual terrine by carefully placing all the ingredients so that when it is sliced it looks like a slab of marble.

I won't pretend, however, that it is a quick dish to make, because all the ingredients have to be prepared meticulously, then layered in the terrine quite precisely, if you want them to have the full effect. We even cook the carrot slices that wrap the terrine and the cabbage leaves which are incorporated into it in the duck fat, so that the confit character infuses the entire terrine; alternatively, you can simply blanch them, as here. If you find items like lamb tongues and duck gizzards difficult to obtain, you can simply substitute the meat from confit duck legs.

serves 10-12

for the terrine:

4 large carrots, the biggest you can find, plus 6 medium carrots

freshly ground salt and pepper

a little olive oil

4 large Savoy cabbage leaves

2 lamb knuckles, cooked as described on page 107, meat stripped from the bone

250 g cassoulet beans, cooked as described opposite

10 g basil, chopped

10 g thyme, chopped

10 g tarragon, chopped

250 g cured foie gras, cut into cubes

200 ml lamb stock

4 gelatine leaves, soaked in cold water

for the Confit:

900 g smoked belly bacon or pancetta

10 lamb tongues, blanched (optional)

10 duck gizzards (optional)

4 Morteaux (smoked coarse pork) sausages

4 Toulouse sausages

2 onions, halved

2 carrots, halved

6 garlic cloves, lightly crushed

2 sprigs of thyme

4 bay leaves

750 g duck or goose fat, melted

for the garnish:

100 g baby onions

100 g carrots, finely diced

100 g cassoulet beans, cooked as described opposite

2 tomatoes

200 ml sherry vinegar

100 g goose fat, melted

3 tbsp truffle oil

450 ml vegetable oil

4 garlic cloves, chopped

handful of tarragon, chopped

50 g chopped chives

The day before you want to serve:

1 First confit the meats: preheat the oven to 150°C/300°F/gas 2. Put the belly bacon, lamb tongues and duck gizzards if you are using them, and both types of sausage in an ovenproof pan with the onion, carrot, garlic, thyme and bay leaves. Cover with the duck or goose fat and leave in the oven for 2 hours.

2 Meanwhile, prepare the vegetables for the terrine: peel and slice the large carrots thinly lengthwise, preferably using a mandoline slicer. Put the strips of raw carrot into a large bowl, season and add a little olive oil. Reserve.

3 Blanch the cabbage leaves in boiling salted water for 1 minute, drain, refresh in cold water, drain well again and reserve.

4 Cook the medium carrots in boiling salted water until just tender and reserve.

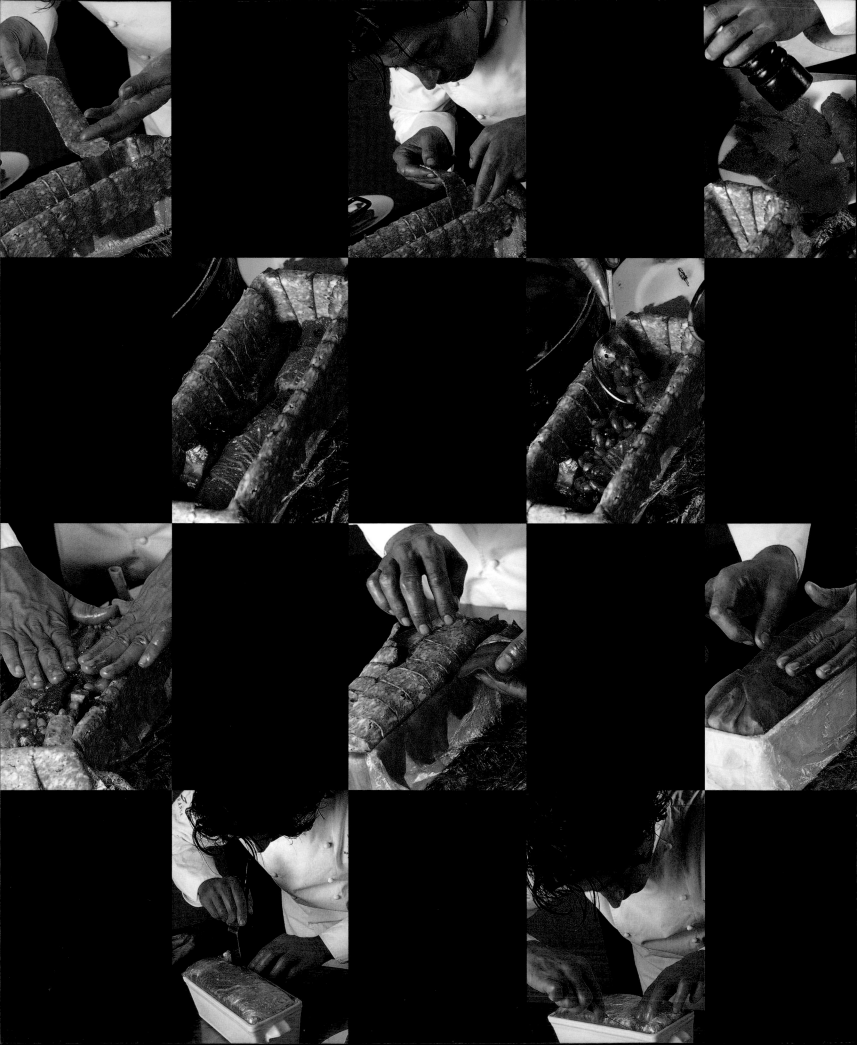

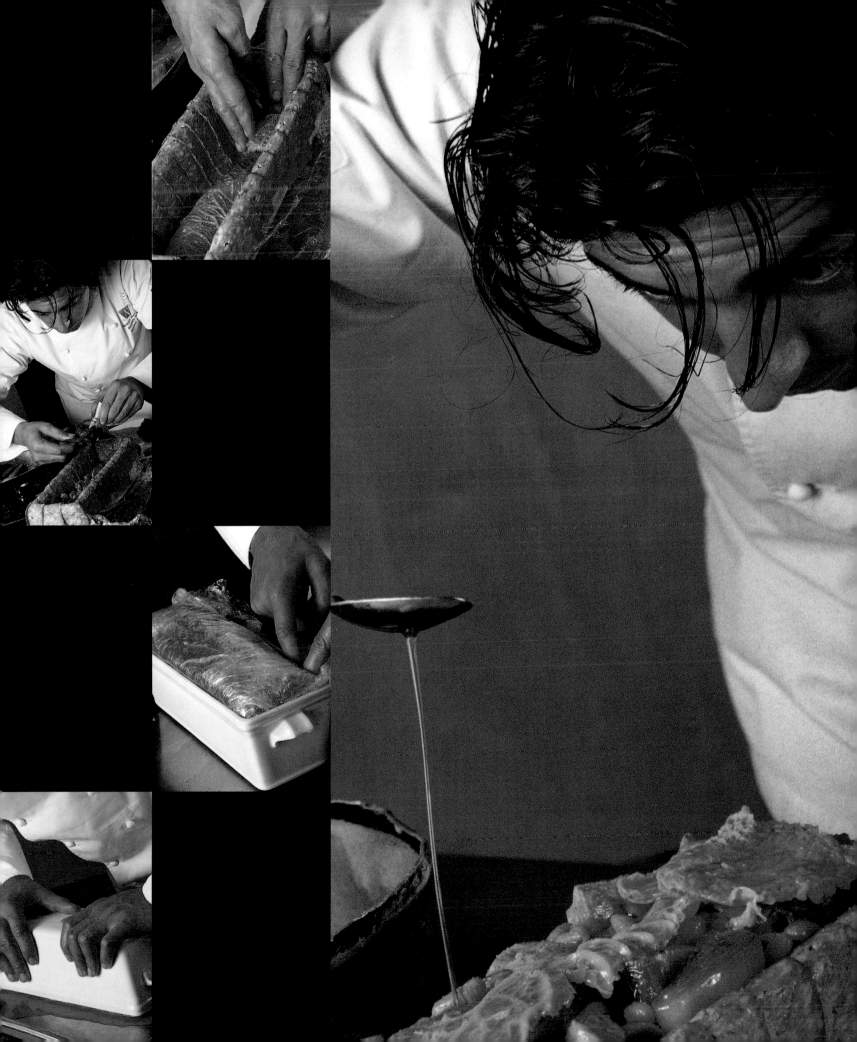

5 When the confit meats are cooked: remove them from the oven and leave to cool slightly in the pan. Take out two of the Morteaux sausages and reserve. Halve the belly bacon or pancetta lengthwise.

6 Peel the lamb tongues and put them back into the pan of meats.

7 Add the cooked medium carrots, cassoulet beans and herbs to the pan of meats.

8 Slice the two reserved Morteaux sausages thinly lengthwise, put them into a separate bowl, season and add a little olive oil.

9 Season the cabbage leaves.

10 To assemble the terrine: line a large terrine with three layers of cling-film, leaving an overhang of about 20 cm over each side to wrap over the top once filled.

11 Line the cling-film with the strips of carrot, overlapping them slightly, so there are no gaps and again leaving an overhang all round to pull over the top of the terrine when filled.

12 Repeat using the strips of Morteaux sausage.

13 Place two of the Toulouse sausages end to end along the bottom right-hand side of the terrine.

14 Spoon in a line of lamb knuckle meat, using half of it, along the other side.

15 Sprinkle some cassoulet beans over the top.

16 Place a row of lamb tongues and half the gizzards on top, plus a slice of belly bacon or pancetta.

17 Position the cooked carrots on top and scatter on more beans.

18 Follow with a line of the remaining lamb knuckle meat.

19 Wrap the remaining Morteaux sausages in the cabbage leaves and place end to end on top of the lamb. Sprinkle with more beans.

20 Finish with a row of the remaining gizzards, belly bacon or pancetta and the two remaining Toulouse sausages placed end to end. Top with foie gras and sprinkle the remaining beans over the top.

21 Heat the lamb stock in a pan, add the drained and squeezed-out gelatine leaves and whisk well to dissolve the gelatine thoroughly. Allow to cool slightly, then pour over the terrine.

22 Pull the inner layer of sausage over the top of the terrine, then the final layer of carrot. Pull the overhanging layers of cling-film over the top, tucking in the opposite side with a

palette knife. Repeat all the way round.

23 Cut a piece of thick cardboard to fit the top of the terrine. Press down, then wrap the entire terrine as tightly as possible in cling-film, place something heavy on top and leave in the fridge for at least 24 hours.

next day, when ready to serve:

24 Make the garnish: blanch the baby onions and diced carrots for about 1 minute in boiling water, drain, refresh in cold water, drain again and put in a bowl with the cassoulet beans.

25 Blanch the tomatoes briefly in boiling water, pop into a bowl of cold water, then remove the skin, quarter, scrape out the seeds and dice the flesh into $1/2$-cm cubes.

26 Whisk the vinegar, goose fat, truffle oil and vegetable oil together, and season well.

27 Add one-third of this dressing to the bowl of cassoulet beans, together with the diced tomato, chopped garlic, tarragon and chives. Season again to taste.

28 To serve: pour a little of the remaining dressing in the centre of each plate. Place a thin slice of terrine on top and brush with a little more dressing. Spoon the dressed beans around the outside.

'You take the idea of a hot rustic cassoulet and transform it into a soft, yielding cold marbled terrine.'

rabbit

For many years rabbit was a very unappreciated meat, but recently it has become very fashionable. Unlike much game meat, it has a very delicate flavour, which means it is often used in a similar way to chicken. French rabbits tend to be much bigger than the ones you find in England, and the best are the wild rabbits known as *garenne*, from the French for 'warren'. Rabbit also makes good confit and rillettes (see pages 74-5).

Confit of Rabbit Leg with Vanilla-seed Risotto

This is a simple version of a dish devised by my good friend and Novelli Group Executive Chef, Richard Guest, who has been with me since the days at The Four Seasons. According to him, he was looking for a smooth ingredient to take the savoury flavour of the rabbit through into a gentle sweetness, but yet avoid masking the delicate taste of the meat with a sharp or overpowering sauce. Vanilla fitted the purpose perfectly. To make it simpler, instead of the confit rabbit legs you could pan-fry some slices of rabbit loin, following the method in the recipe for the restaurant dish that follows.

serves 4

4 confit rabbit legs, prepared and cooked as
   described for duck legs on page 74
200 ml veal or chicken jus

for the Vanilla Seed Risotto:

a little olive oil
3 shallots, finely chopped
1 garlic clove, crushed
1 vanilla pod, split lengthwise
100 g risotto rice
100 ml sweet white wine
300 ml hot chicken or rabbit stock
10 g butter
1 tbsp mascarpone
10 g grated Parmesan cheese
1 tsp chopped chives
freshly ground salt and pepper
4 sprigs of chervil, to garnish

1 Preheat the oven to 190°C/375°F/gas 5.

2 Make the risotto: heat a little olive oil in a deep pan and sweat the shallots and garlic with the vanilla pod over a low heat, until softened but not coloured.

3 Add the rice and stir until well coated. Add the wine and cook, stirring all the time, until the wine has been absorbed by the rice.

4 Add the hot stock very slowly, stirring with each addition, until all the stock has been absorbed and the rice is soft.

5 Fold in the butter, mascarpone and Parmesan. Add the chopped chives and season to taste. Remove the vanilla pod and reserve. Cover the risotto and keep warm.

6 Put the legs into an ovenproof dish with the veal or chicken jus and cook in the oven for 5–10 minutes, basting regularly, until the meat takes on a rich colour and shine. Remove from the oven and keep warm.

7 Place the rabbit legs in the centres of the serving plates and spoon the risotto around them. Garnish with chervil and the reserved vanilla.

'Smooth vanilla takes the savoury flavour of the rabbit into a gentle sweetness.'

Rabbit and Vanilla-seed Risotto with Confit Rabbit Leg, Rabbit Loin and Vanilla Sauce

This is Richard Guest's dish as it appears on the menu at Maison Novelli. We use red shiso, an Oriental herb, to garnish the dish. The leaves have a slightly aniseed flavour, not unlike chervil, but since their main function is decoration, don't worry if you can't find them.

serves 4

Vanilla-seed Risotto (as previous page)
a little olive oil
freshly ground salt and pepper
4 rabbit loins
4 confit rabbit legs, prepared and cooked as
   described for duck legs on page 74
200 ml veal or chicken jus

for the Vanilla Sauce:

200 ml Muscat dessert wine
1 vanilla pod, split lengthwise
1 garlic clove, lightly crushed
1 tsp olive oil

to serve:

a little Basil Oil (page 11)
a few chervil sprigs
red shiso (optional)

1 Preheat the oven to 190°C/375°F/gas 5. First make the risotto as described on the previous page, reserving the vanilla pod and cutting it into 4 strips. Keep warm.

2 Heat a pan and put in a thin film of olive oil. Season the loins and cook them on all sides until golden brown and cooked through, about 6 minutes.

3 Add the strips of vanilla pod discarded from the risotto. Stir around the pan until the seeds from the pods coat the rabbit. Remove the pan from the heat and leave to rest for 3 minutes.

4 Meanwhile, slice the bases from the confit rabbit legs so that they will stand upright, and cook and glaze with the veal or chicken jus as described on the previous page.

5 Make the Vanilla Sauce: put all the ingredients except the olive oil into a small saucepan and bubble up gently, so that the liquid reduces slowly to a syrup. Stir in the olive oil and season.

6 Spoon some risotto into the centre of each plate and place a confit rabbit leg upright in the centre.

7 Carve each rabbit loin into 6-8 slices and arrange these in an overlapping circle on top of the risotto.

8 Drizzle the vanilla sauce around the edge of the plate and intersperse with drops of basil oil and juices from the pan used for glazing the confit rabbit legs.

9 Garnish with the vanilla pod strips used for cooking the rabbit loins, a sprig of chervil and red shiso if you have it.

Daube of beef, pot au feu, braised lamb knuckle, these are all dishes which my mother cooked and my grandmother cooked before her, and the food with which every French person has grown up. When they are made with patience and care they are wonderful meals in themselves, but when I see such timeless dishes they seem to challenge me to take hold of them and reinvent them in some new, unexpected and exciting way.

I see a plain pot au feu and imagine a beautiful terrine made with the tender meat, shot through the centre with green lentils and wrapped in brilliant green cabbage leaves. I see a classic beef daube and I want to combine it with smooth chicken mousse to stuff a boned chicken leg or pig's trotter or a shiny glazed onion...

beef

When you buy the best cuts of beef, you want a good dark colour — indicating the beef has been well hung — with no sinew but a nice marbling of fat throughout the flesh. Sirloin steak should have a good creamy, not too yellow, layer of fat, but rump and fillet should have virtually none.

We always try to buy Aberdeen Angus beef from Scotland, which most chefs agree is the best there is. When you buy ox-cheek for beef daube you may be offered it already lightly salted. Always check, and if this is the case, omit the curing stage of the recipe. However, I firmly believe that it is best to salt your own beef if you can.

Minute Steak Mignonette, Watercress Salad, Béarnaise and Pommes Frites

This is a dish that people make all over the world, but it is most famous as a French brasserie dish, so when I opened my first brasserie in London I knew it would have to be on the menu. Steak frites can often be a disappointment, but when the steak is tender and exactly cooked, the chips are perfectly crisp on the outside and soft inside, and the Béarnaise sauce just piquant, this is a wonderful combination of things to eat.

The same cooking principle you use for pan-frying a scallop or a piece of sea bass applies to fillet steak: first get your pan hot, then put in a thin film of oil and get that very hot too before putting in the steak. When you are cooking a steak rolled in mignonette (mixed peppercorns), to get a really good crunchy crust it is important not to disturb the meat until the moment you flip it over on to the second side, and then not again until you take it out of the pan.

A good steak is also a well seasoned one — you need to add salt and pepper before cooking, or, in this case, add salt before coating with the mignonette. Some chefs prefer not to salt steak before cooking, as they feel it draws out the juices which you want to seal inside. I believe, however, that if you add your salt once the cooking process has started and the surface of the meat is sealed in the hot fat, it will have formed a barrier against the salt, and won't absorb it so well.

Beef Fillet, Wild Mushroom Polenta w[ith]
Cep Oil and Parmesan Crackling

In France you would probably buy a tournedos or
this. These are the very tender round slices cut
you often hear French people call a charming lit

In our restaurant kitchens we wrap whole b
film to form a cylinder, and hang it for a day.
slice off individual portions, cutting through t
left on until the very last moment to keep the s
goes into the pan, we remove the cling-film and
shape as it cooks.

serves 4

16 whole shallots
400 ml melted duck or goose fat
250 g fast-cook polenta
a little olive oil
250 g wild mushrooms, preferably ceps,
    chopped, plus 8 for garnish, quartered
1 shallot, finely chopped
1 garlic clove, finely chopped
50 g mascarpone
50 g foie gras, diced
25 g butter
10 g Parmesan cheese, grated
small bunch of basil leaves, shredded
freshly ground salt and pepper
4 fillet steaks, each about 250 g
a little cep (porcini) oil

to garnish:
more cep (porcini) oil
Parmesan Crackling (see page 118), moulded
    into a wave shape rather than a basket
a little Cep Powder (page 15)

1 Confit the whole sh
cooking in the oven p
and reserve.
2 Turn the oven setti
3 Cook the polenta a
4 Heat a little olive o
chopped shallot and g
5 Mix the contents o
mascarpone and foie
basil. Keep warm.
6 Season the beef all
7 Heat an ovenproof
that very hot. Put in
8 Add the confit shall
remaining knob of bu
6-8 minutes.
9 Remove the pan fr
2-3 minutes. Add a sp
10 To serve: spoon so
roughly. Drizzle with
11 Place a fillet of be
and some of the reser
12 Spoon around a li
wave of Parmesan cra
with cep powder.

4 fillet steaks, each about 175 g
1 tbsp mixed peppercorns
1 tbsp coriander seeds
salt
a little olive oil
4 large bunches of watercress
a little Sherry Dressing (page 11)
Pommes Frites (see page 94)

for the Béarnaise Sauce:
2 egg yolks
1 tbsp white wine
1 tsp tarragon vinegar
1 tbsp chopped tarragon
1 tbsp water
freshly ground salt and pepper
100 g butter, diced

1 Make sure you take the steaks from the
fridge well ahead of cooking to allow them to
come to room temperature, as cooking time is
so brief. Bat the steaks out slightly to
tenderize them.
2 Make the Béarnaise Sauce: place all the
ingredients except the butter in a round-
bottomed bowl and place over a pan of
simmering water. Whisk in a figure-of-eight
motion as fast as possible until the sauce
becomes as thick as whipped cream, then
remove from the heat and slowly whisk in the
butter. If the sauce thickens too much, adjust
it by whisking in a spoonful of hot water.
Season to taste, and keep warm. Do not allow
to boil or the sauce will separate.
3 To make the mignonette: crush the
peppercorns and coriander seeds and put
through a fine sieve. Discard the fine powder,
as this will be too fiery. Season the steaks with
salt and then press the crushed mignonette
into both sides of each steak.
4 Heat a heavy pan until very hot, then add
the oil and heat until that is very hot. Seal the
steaks in it for 1 minute on each side.

5 Dress the watercress with the sherry dressing.
6 Serve the steak with the watercress, pommes
frites and Béarnaise sauce.

pomme
frite

As I always say about using all your sense
chip sing at the point at which it is reac
my first job at a bistro in Arras. I was t
a job you might think, but even making chi

The two big disappointments with chi
good on the outside but aren't cooked in t
simply to blanch the chips first to part-c
temperature and cook again for just long e
overcooking it all the way through.

Don't cook too many at one go, or yo
you add the chips. Instead cook in batches

1 Peel some large waxy potatoes and cut
each potato into slices about 1 cm thick,
then cut these into strips 1.5 cm wide.
Try to make sure the chips are of an equal
size, otherwise the thinner ones will cook
more quickly.
2 Fill your deep-fryer with oil or half-fill a
chip pan (never fill it further) and heat the
oil to 150°C.

3 Lower the
not using a f
blanch for al
are just soft
but not colo
4 Remove th
kitchen pape
5 Just befor
reheat the oi

beef daub

Beef daube was put on the menu by Jean-Marie Lenfant, one of the original
loyal band of chefs who came with me from The Four Seasons and helped to
up Maison Novelli. I was bursting with ambition and ideas, but I only had
few pounds left in my back pocket after I had done the deal over the
restaurant.

Jean-Marie manfully tested recipes and ran the tiny kitchen of the
brasserie on the ground floor, with Richard Guest working upstairs in the
restaurant kitchen. When we weren't serving customers, the two of them we
up ladders helping me to paint the walls, laying tiles or arranging flowe

Now Jean-Marie is running Le Moulin de Jean, the mill I bought in
Normandy, which is only about 20 kilometres from the farm whe
his family grow or rear most of their own produce
including rabbits. They even make th
own Calvados, cider and
Cassis. Jean-Marie's
mother loves to feed
people and this is th
way she and generation
of excellent French
country cooks like her
would half-cure and cook
daube de boeuf.

The important thing is
cook the dish for the first
part only in wine, which mus
be a rich mature wine, nothi
too young or it will give the
dish a sour taste. Only when t
meat has taken up the flavour o
the wine do you add stock.

When I began to think about
ideas for the menu at Les Saveurs
mind turned to ways of presenting
daube, beyond using it to stuff chi
legs and pigs' trotters, dishes whic
already had on the menu at Maison No
and Novelli W8. I came up with the re
for richly glazed onions, stuffed with
daube, which follows.

Half-cured Beef Daube

serves 4

4 ox cheeks or 1 kg top rump or chuck beef

1 kg rock salt

2 celery stalks, chopped

2 carrots, chopped

2 onions, chopped

1 head of garlic, halved through the middle

500 ml robust red wine

250 ml Madeira

250 ml port

freshly ground salt and black pepper

a little flour

a little olive oil

100 g belly pork, chopped

pared rind from 1 orange

4 sprigs each of thyme and rosemary

4 bay leaves

1 litre beef stock

knob of butter

2 tbsp liquorice essence

the day before:

1 Trim all the skin and fat from the meat. Cover with the salt and leave for 6 hours, turning regularly.

2 Rinse the meat, put in a large bowl, together with the vegetables and garlic, and pour in the wine, Madeira and port. Cover the bowl with cling-film and leave to marinate in the fridge for 24 hours.

next day:

3 Remove the meat and vegetables, reserving the marinade. Pat the meat dry and dust it in a little seasoned flour.

4 Heat some oil in a large heavy-based ovenproof pan and brown the meat all over. Add the vegetables and sauté for a little longer, until lightly coloured.

5 In a separate pan, boil up the marinade and skim.

6 Add the marinade to the pan with the meat and vegetables, together with the belly pork, orange rind and herbs. Cook very slowly on top of the stove for 1 hour.

7 Meanwhile, preheat the oven to 160ºC/325ºF/gas 3.

8 Add the stock to the pan, cover and transfer to the oven for 4 hours. The beef is ready when it falls apart readily when a fork is inserted into it. Remove the meat from its cooking liquor and keep warm.

9 Strain the liquor through a fine sieve into a clean pan and bubble up until reduced to a sauce-like consistency.

10 To finish the sauce, wave in the butter and liquorice.

11 Slice the meat and serve with the sauce and potato or celeriac purée (overleaf).

Sweet Glazed Onion Stuffed with Beef Daube

We use sweet Saint-André onions for this recipe.

serves 4

4 large sweet white onions (as large as you can find)

600 ml red wine

600 ml veal jus

½ recipe quantity Beef Daube (as on the previous page)

a little olive oil

100 g foie gras, roughly chopped

300 g shallots, chopped finely

4 garlic cloves, crushed

50 g basil, shredded

freshly ground salt and pepper

for the Celeriac Purée:

1 large celeriac, roughly chopped

1 large potato, roughly chopped

1 garlic clove, chopped

about 600 ml milk

25 g butter

a drop of truffle oil (optional)

for the Mixed Mushrooms:

a little olive oil

300 g assorted wild mushrooms

1 garlic clove, chopped

50 g basil, shredded

1 Preheat the oven to 160°C/325°F/gas 3. Peel the outer layer from the onions.

2 Put the red wine and veal jus in a large pan and bring to a simmer. Add the onions and poach gently until just soft. Remove the onions from the pan, reserving the liquid.

3 Carefully, going in from the top, pull out the onion hearts, leaving a good thick exterior to hold the stuffing, and chop the onion hearts quite finely.

4 Chop the beef daube quite finely.

5 Heat a little olive oil in a pan, add the chopped beef, chopped onion, foie gras, shallots, garlic and basil with some seasoning and sauté for a few minutes.

6 Carefully stuff each onion with this mixture.

7 Place the onions in a roasting pan, pour around the reserved cooking liquid and spoon some over each onion.

8 Roast in the oven for about 30-40 minutes, basting regularly until the onions are glazed and golden brown.

9 While the onions are roasting, make the celeriac purée: put the celeriac and potato in a pan with the garlic and enough milk to cover. Season. Simmer until the vegetables are very soft to the touch, then drain off three-quarters of the milk.

10 Add the butter and whiz in a blender until smooth. Season again to taste, add a drop of truffle oil if you like (just a drop, or it will be overpowering) and keep warm.

11 Sauté the Mixed Mushrooms: heat a little olive oil in a pan, add the mushrooms, garlic and basil and sauté very briefly until coloured.

12 To serve: place the stuffed onion in the centre of the plate and surround with the celeriac purée and mushrooms.

Pot au feu is one of the oldest dishes in France, and this recipe is quite faithful to the classic recipe, though I like to add a little truffle oil at the end! Like many such meal-in-a-pot dishes, pot au feu traditionally fulfilled many roles: the cooking broth could be served with croutons, the meat and vegetables eaten separately, and any leftover meat made into a salad or kept for meatballs or a meatloaf the next day.

It is this last notion that first inspired me to make my spin-off dish of pork knuckle and lentil terrine. One day, when I was at The Provence Restaurant in Lymington, Hampshire, we had a big party booked. They had asked for pot au feu, and then cancelled too late for me to stop my meat order, so I was left with a kitchen full of pork hocks. The staff were complaining that they were forever eating casseroles and stews, so I decided to cook the hocks and then make them into a terrine as a change for them. It turned out so well that we decided to develop the terrine further to serve to the customers, adding the lentils, baby onions and shiitake mushrooms and wrapping the whole thing in cabbage leaves.

Pot au Feu

serves 4

2 pork hocks

2 onions

2 celery stalks

10 black peppercorns

3 bay leaves

1 sprig of thyme, roughly chopped

1 small Savoy cabbage, roughly cut up

2 small potatoes (turned, if you like, into barrel shapes)

1 small swede

2 small leeks, trimmed and halved

3 carrots, halved

2 garlic cloves, split in half

6 basil leaves, chopped

freshly ground salt and pepper

to serve:

rock salt

a little truffle oil (optional)

a little mustard and cress

a little flat-leaved parsley

the day before:

1 Soak the pork hocks in cold water overnight to remove any excess salt.

next day, at least 4 hours before you want to serve:

2 Rinse the hocks well and put them in a pan with one of the onions and one of the celery stalks, roughly chopped, the peppercorns, bay leaves and thyme. Cover with water and simmer for about 3 hours until tender, skimming and topping up with water as necessary. The oldest and best way to test that the meat is correctly cooked is to pull the small bone at the top of the hock, known as the *souris* or 'mouse'. If it comes away, then the meat is ready.

3 Remove the hocks from the pan, reserving the liquid. Strain this cooking liquid and bring it back to the boil, then

add the remaining onion and celery stalk, halved, together with the rest of the vegetables, the garlic and basil leaves. Cook until the vegetables are tender.

4 Remove bones and excess fat from the meat and put it in the pan with the vegetables to heat through. Adjust seasoning.

5 To serve: pile the meat in the centre of the plates, arrange the vegetables around the meat and pour over a little of the cooking stock. Sprinkle with rock salt and, if you like, drizzle over a little truffle oil. Garnish with mustard and cress and parsley.

Cabbage-wrapped Pork Knuckle Terrine with Sauce Gribiche

serves 10

125 g baby onions, peeled

6 large Savoy cabbage leaves

a little duck fat

5 pork hocks, cooked as for pot au feu on
  page 100

500 ml cooking liquor from the hocks

olive oil

500 g shiitake mushrooms

1 garlic clove, crushed

1 tbsp clear honey

sprigs of dill, to garnish

for the Green Lentils:

100 g dried green lentils

2 shallots, finely chopped

1 small carrot, finely chopped

1 celery stalk, finely chopped

2 garlic cloves, crushed

1 bay leaf

4 plum tomatoes

6 basil leaves, chopped

a dash of sherry vinegar

1 tbsp truffle oil

freshly ground salt and pepper

for the Sauce Gribiche:

250 ml olive oil

1 bunch each of tarragon, parsley and dill

50 g capers

1 tsp white wine vinegar

whites of 3 hard-boiled eggs, chopped

well ahead, ideally 2 days ahead of serving:

1 Put the lentils to soak in water overnight. Proper soaking helps the skins to stay on during cooking.

next day:

2 Prepare the lentils: drain them and put them in a pan with the shallots, carrot, celery, garlic and bay leaf. Cover with some of the cooking liquor from the hocks and bring to the boil, then turn down the heat and simmer until the lentils are soft to the touch, about 20 minutes. Drain the lentils and leave to cool.

3 Blanch the tomatoes briefly in boiling water, then peel, deseed and chop the flesh. Mix the tomatoes, basil, sherry vinegar and truffle oil into the lentils and season to taste. Reserve.

4 While the lentils are cooking, blanch the baby onions for about 1 minute in boiling water, drain and reserve.

5 Season the cabbage leaves. Put a little duck fat into a pan and fry them until soft. Remove and reserve.

6 Remove all the bones, fat and sinew from the pork hocks and reserve the meat.

7 Reduce the remaining cooking liquor from the hocks until it is syrupy. Mix the pork meat with a little of this syrup and season with pepper.

8 Heat a little olive oil in a pan and briefly sauté the shiitake mushrooms and garlic. Reserve.

9 Heat the honey in a pan and cook the baby onions slowly in it until they caramelize. Reserve.

10 Lay 3 layers of cling-film on a work surface, one on top of the other. Cover the cling-film with a rectangle of cabbage leaves, about 40 x 25cm, overlapping to leave no gaps. Cover the cabbage leaves with the pork mixture, leaving a little clear gap at the edges.

11 Mix together the mushrooms, baby onions and lentils. Spoon the mixture in a strip down the centre of the pork mixture.

12 Roll up carefully and tightly like a Swiss roll inside the cling-film. Twist the ends together tightly, wrap in another layer of cling-film and chill overnight.

On the day of serving:

13 Make the Sauce Gribiche: in a blender or food processor, blitz together all the ingredients except the egg white. Press through a fine sieve, then mix in the egg white and season to taste.

14 Turn out the terrine, unwrap and slice thickly. Brush each side of each slice with olive oil.

15 To serve: place a slice of terrine in the centre of each plate and spoon some sauce around the outside. Garnish with dill and season with freshly ground black pepper.

pigs' trotters

Surprisingly for a Frenchman, I had never cooked a pig's trotter in my life until Marco Pierre White showed me how to prepare trotters in the style of Pierre Koffmann. One of the most important things is to bone them correctly, so that you don't puncture the skin.

Once I had the technique, I started developing my own version of pigs' trotters, cooked 'suivant mon humeur', adding extra ingredients, according to my mood. I became crazy about pigs' trotters, cooking them again and again, until they became better and better and more and more full of flavour. To alleviate the boredom of boning, sometimes, fifty trotters at a time, we set up a competition in the kitchen to see who could do it the fastest. At first I held the record, then Richard Guest took over, with a time of 30 seconds for a single trotter!

To the basic chicken mousse stuffing, I add sautéed black pudding and beef daube. Sometimes I also put in Toulouse sausage which has been poached, skinned, diced and then fried. I might even add some sautéed wild mushrooms and foie gras or some confit ox tongue or Morteaux sausage. On another day I might add some pork from a *pot au feu*. The important thing to remember is that whatever you add must be cooked first, because the trotters are only steamed for about 12 minutes, long enough to cook the mousse, but not any other raw ingredients.

serves 4

4 hind-leg pigs' trotters, shin bone removed

1 onion, chopped

2 carrots, chopped

2 celery stalks, chopped

1 leek, chopped

5 garlic cloves, chopped

200 ml each white and red wine

a little butter

400 ml veal jus, reduced to a syrup

4 sprigs of thyme

4 bay leaves

Celeriac Purée (page 98), to serve

1 tbsp truffle oil

freshly ground salt and pepper

for the stuffing:
see Spit-roast Chicken Leg (page 67)

1 First prepare the trotters: singe off the hairs from the skin, either using a blow-torch or by holding the trotter with a fork over a flame.

2 Place the trotters pad-side down on your work surface. Using a sharp knife, make a lengthwise slit down the centre. Using the knife to help you, strip and peel away the skin and flesh like a glove, taking care not to rip the skin and working as close to the bone as possible, to expose it completely. Cut through the knuckle joint, then twist and crack off the top of the bone to expose the knuckle bone. Leave this in, as it will be easier to remove later.

3 Put the trotters into a large heavy-based pan with the vegetables, garlic and wines, adding enough water to cover, and simmer gently for 1½ hours, until the trotters are soft to the touch.

4 Meanwhile, preheat the oven to 150ºC/300ºF/gas 2. Put the trotters in a roasting pan. Reserve the cooking liquor.

5 Strain the cooking liquor through a fine sieve into a clean pan and bubble up until reduced by two-thirds. Add the reduced veal jus.

6 Season the trotters in the pan and pour over the cooking liquor. Cook in the oven for at least 6 hours, basting regularly until the trotters are

dark brown and shiny and the cooking liquor has reduced down almost to nothing.

7 Meanwhile, prepare the stuffing as described on page 67.

8 Remove the trotters from the oven and when cool enough to handle place pad side down on your work surface. Pull out the knuckle bone.

9 For each trotter, take three large squares of foil and place one on top of the other. Grease the top square thoroughly with butter. Lay a sprig of thyme and a bay leaf on it. Lay a trotter on top, with the intact skin side down.

10 Open up the trotter like a purse and spoon in enough stuffing to fill it out to its original shape. Pull the edges of the skin together to enclose the stuffing and roll up very tightly in the foil, twisting the ends to resemble a Christmas cracker.

11 Put into a steamer and steam for about 12 minutes, until heated right through.

12 Very carefully unwrap the trotters, leaving the herbs in place, and put them on warmed plates, intact skin-side up. Serve with celeriac purée, drizzle truffle oil and the remaining cooking liquor around and season.

lamb

Being French, it is natural for me to cook with every part of an animal. It would be very easy to use only prime fillets of lamb, but for me it is hard to beat the tender, melting meat that comes from a lamb knuckle, simmered slowly then braised in a sauce made of its own stock and enriched with honey, to give it a wonderful shiny glaze.

The knuckle is the part of the lamb below the shoulder (or sometimes the thigh) and above the foot. Butchers normally take the knuckle bone away, leaving the meat to form part of the shoulder, so you may have to ask your butcher to keep some whole knuckles for you.

In summer I like to marinate the knuckles and then barbecue them, just as you might cook an overgrown chicken drumstick; they are also delicious braised, then coated in breadcrumbs mixed with herbs and spices and spit-roasted. The braised knuckle can be served quite simply with some mashed potatoes and seasonal vegetables, or the Chickpea Salsa opposite. Alternatively, you can dress it up as we do in the restaurant, by adding Pommes Carlos and a Masala Sauce (see page 108).

Classic Braised Lamb Knuckle in Stock

serves 4

4 medium lamb knuckles or shanks

a little oil

freshly ground salt and black pepper

2 carrots, cut into chunks

2 onions, cut into chunks

2 leeks, cut into chunks

225 g celeriac, cut into chunks

1 head of garlic, broken up

handful of mixed rosemary, bay and thyme

juice of 1/2 lemon

2 tsp honey

for the sauce:

20 g sliced shallots

10 g sliced celery

20 g sliced button mushrooms

25 g unsalted butter

1 tbsp finely chopped fresh mixed herbs
   preferably including tarragon, parsley and
   basil

250 ml red wine

1 Remove excess fat from the knuckles and trim the meat away to expose a length of bone. Reserve the meat trimmings.

2 Heat a little oil in a roasting pan on the hob. Season the knuckles and add to the pan with the vegetables. Brown them quickly all over.

3 While they brown, bring a large pan of salted water to the boil then plunge the knuckles in it for 1-2 minutes. This 'blanching' helps the meat to retract around the bone and keep it in one piece during cooking.

4 Drain and put in a clean pan with the vegetables, garlic and herbs, together with enough water to cover the meat. Bring to the boil, lower the heat and simmer gently for about 1½ hours, to the point where the meat is almost falling off the bone. Remove the knuckles from the stock and keep warm. Reserve the stock.

5 Make the sauce: preheat the oven to 160°C/325°F/gas 3. Sweat the sliced vegetables in a little of the butter to soften them without browning them. Add the reserved lamb trimmings and the mixed herbs and cook for a further 2-3 minutes.

6 Pour in the red wine and bubble until reduced by half. Add 500 ml of the reserved lamb stock and reduce again by half.

7 Cut the remaining butter into small pieces and whisk these in, a few at a time. Season to taste and pass through a fine sieve.

8 Pour half of this sauce into a roasting pan. Stir in the lemon juice and honey. Add the knuckles and coat with this glaze. Cook in the oven for about 20 minutes, removing every 5 minutes to baste the knuckles.

9 To serve: remove the knuckles from the roasting pan and keep warm. Add the remaining sauce to the pan and heat through. Pass through a fine sieve. Place each knuckle on a warmed plate, pour on a little sauce. Serve with mashed potatoes and vegetables of choice.

Chickpea Salsa

200 g chickpeas

2 medium tomatoes

a little oil

1 small onion, finely diced

2 garlic cloves, finely diced

1 large carrot, finely diced

1 celery stalk, finely diced

1 bay leaf

1 sprig of thyme

600 ml lamb stock

freshly ground salt and pepper

10 basil leaves, shredded

50 g capers, rinsed and drained

the day before:

1 Soak the chickpeas overnight in water.

next day:

2 Make tomato concassé by blanching, skinning, deseeding and dicing the tomatoes (see page 24). Set aside.

3 Heat a little oil in a pan and sauté the onion, garlic, carrots and celery gently for a few minutes. Add bay leaf and thyme.

4 Drain the chickpeas and add to the pan, followed by the tomatoes. Pour in the lamb stock and add water to cover. Cook very gently until the chickpeas are tender and the liquid absorbed (anything from 45 minutes to 4 hours), topping up with water as necessary. Season.

5 Just before serving as a bed for the lamb, stir in the basil and capers.

Honey-glazed Lamb Knuckle with Confit Vegetables, Pommes Carlos and Spicy Masala Sauce

In the brasserie we serve this dish in shallow bowls, with confit vegetables surrounding the lamb knuckle and the bone decorated with a fried bay leaf and Pommes Carlos — a potato flower made from wafer-thin slices of potato.

serves 4

4 lamb knuckles, cooked and glazed as on the
   previous page but without the final sauce

for the Pommes Carlos:

4 medium potatoes, turned into oval shapes
a little salted butter, melted

for the garnish:

16 shallots
16 shiitake mushrooms
8 baby carrots
4 celery stalks, halved lengthwise
about 600 ml melted duck or goose fat
8 cherry tomatoes
a little olive oil
4 fresh bay leaves
4 sprigs of chervil

for the Masala Spice Mix:

1 tbsp each ground ginger; cardamom, cumin,
   caraway, coriander and mustard seeds;
   cayenne pepper; black and white peppercorns
6 cloves
2 tsp each cinnamon, garam masala and salt
2 tbsp turmeric
sprig of curry leaves
3 pieces of cassia bark

for the Masala Sauce:

25g butter
6 onions, very thinly sliced
4 garlic cloves, crushed
4 tomatoes, chopped
600 ml chicken stock
300 ml double cream
10g chopped coriander
juice of 1 lime

1 First make the Pommes Carlos: preheat the oven to 130°C/275°/gas 1 and slice each potato very thinly (preferably with a mandoline). Arrange on a non-stick baking tray in overlapping circles to resemble flowers (leaving a hole in the centre) and brush with melted butter.

2 Cover with a sheet of baking parchment, weight down and leave in the oven for 1 hour. Remove from the oven for 30 minutes (leaving the oven on), then return to the oven and leave until slightly transparent, about 10 minutes. Take out of the oven and leave for 2 minutes to crisp up before lifting off with a spatula.

3 Prepare the vegetables for the garnish: confit the shallots, mushrooms, carrots and celery in the goose fat following the instructions for shallots on page 93.

4 Prepare the lamb knuckles as on the previous page but, as the bones will become a feature, wrap them in foil before you put the knuckles in the oven to keep them white.

5 Make the Masala Sauce: dry roast 2 tablespoons of the masala spice mix briefly in a pan over a low heat to release their flavours (keep the rest in a screw-top jar for other recipes). Put through a coffee grinder and grind until fine.

6 Heat a little butter in another pan and sweat the onions, garlic, tomatoes and 1 tablespoon of the spice mix very slowly until the onions are very soft.

7 Add the stock and bubble up to reduce slowly by about two-thirds.

8 Add the second tablespoon of spice mix and the cream and cook for 15 minutes over a low heat.

9 Put through a fine sieve and add the coriander, lime juice and seasoning. Keep warm and add the cherry tomatoes for garnish to the sauce to warm them through.

10 Heat a little olive oil in a pan and briefly fry the bay leaves to enhance their colour and give a translucent effect.

11 To serve: place a knuckle on each plate, pour on the sauce and surround with confit vegetables and cherry tomatoes. Slide a Pommes Carlos on the end of each knuckle bone and insert a fried bay leaf into the end of the bone. Secure if necessary with a cocktail stick. Garnish with chervil.

veget

I believe that the job of
a chef is to extract as many flavours as
possible from a wide range of ingredients and
that means working with meat and fish and
vegetables. I love all vegetables, particularly
aubergines, ripe sweet tomatoes and fennel ...
and they are at the core of many of my dishes.
Sometimes I am so pleased with the flavours
that I add no meat or fish — for instance,
the goats' cheese terrine with aubergine and
red pepper caviar — but I do not set out to
create vegetarian dishes. I have not been
trained to cook that way. I think that to
cook well, you have to cook what you like
to eat yourself. What lifts you above
the pressures of the kitchen is the joy
of creating something that excites your
own tastebuds. So if I make a gazpacho
soup I cannot help visualizing it with
a tian of crab; a pea soup with a
little foie gras, a crêpe filled
with wild mushrooms bound in
chicken mousse...

Pea Soup with Pancetta

This is another very simple soup which can be made more elaborate when you feel like it, by adding foie gras and a cappuccino topping. By crisping up the pancetta before adding it to the soup, you add a lovely smokiness.

serves 4

a little butter

1 small onion, chopped

50 g pancetta, chopped

400 g fresh or frozen peas

1 garlic clove, roughly chopped

750 ml light chicken stock

1 sprig of mint

freshly ground salt and pepper

pinch of unrefined caster sugar

1 Heat a little butter in a large pan, add the onion and sweat gently until translucent.

2 Get a frying pan very hot, add the pancetta and quickly fry until crisp.

3 Add the pancetta to the other pan, together with the peas and garlic, and cook for a few minutes.

4 Pour in the stock and bring to a simmer. Cook until the peas are soft to the touch. Add the mint, season and add the sugar.

5 Blend until smooth, then put through a fine sieve and serve hot.

Pea and Cured Foie Gras Cappuccino Soup

serves 4

75 g preserved foie gras

freshly ground salt and black pepper

Pea Soup with Pancetta (above)

4 tbsp milk, crème fraîche or cream, warmed through in a pan

25 g unsalted butter

Cep Powder (page 15)

1 Lay the foie gras on a sheet of cling-film and season, then roll up very tightly and chill until firm.

2 Reheat the soup and adjust the seasoning if necessary. Warm 4 soup terrines.

3 When ready to serve the soup, slice the foie gras into rounds about 1½ cm thick. Remove the cling-film.

4 Place a disc of foie gras in the bottom of each of the terrines. Pour the soup on top.

5 If you have a cappuccino frother, froth up 4 tablespoons of warm milk with the butter; if not, whisk some warm cream or crème fraîche with the butter using a hand-held blender. Spoon on top of the bowls.

6 Dust the tops with cep powder to make the soup resemble a large cappuccino.

aubergines

Along with tomatoes, aubergines are among my favourite vegetables. Though some people say you don't need to salt them before cooking, I prefer to, to draw out any bitterness. Just halve them or cut them into chunks if you are making aubergine caviar (see below), put them on a plate, and sprinkle well with rock salt. Leave them for half an hour, then wipe with kitchen paper before cooking.

It is important to season aubergine well before you cook it, as it soaks up seasoning in much the same way as it takes in olive oil. Once the aubergine is cooked and oily it is very difficult to get the seasoning to penetrate.

Aubergine Caviar

This is a classic way of cooking aubergine. The technique takes its name from the aubergine seeds, which look a little like fish eggs when the flesh is cooked. Most chefs purée the cooked aubergine, which enhances the caviar effect, but I prefer to serve it in chunks. That way it makes a great base for dishes such as Andalouse of Sole (see page 50).

It is best to choose slim aubergines, as these have fewer seeds and less of a bitter aftertaste than the fatter, germinating aubergines. They also cook quicker. I have given a cooking time of somewhere between 30 minutes and one hour, which will vary according to the size of the aubergines you buy.

You can make aubergine caviar and store it in a sealed jar in the fridge for up to two weeks, provided it is completely covered in the olive oil in which it has been cooked (top this up with extra olive oil if necessary).

serves 2 as a side dish

1 aubergine

freshly ground salt and black pepper

5 bay leaves

a few basil sprigs

1 sprig of rosemary

1 sprig of thyme

1 whole head of garlic, halved

3 shallots, chopped

pinch of unrefined caster sugar

a little olive oil

1 Preheat the oven to 190ºC/375ºF/gas 5.

2 Cut the aubergine into slices about 2.5 cm thick and salt them as described above.

3 Wipe the aubergine slices to remove excess salt and place them in the centre of a large piece of foil, together with the herbs, garlic and shallots. Season well, sprinkle with sugar and drizzle with the oil, then fold up the foil to make a loose parcel, crimping the edges to seal.

4 Bake in the preheated oven for 30 minutes to 1 hour, until the aubergine flesh is like jelly. Use as an accompaniment to meat or fish, or as required in other recipes.

On holiday in the Pays Basque many years ago I first ate pipérade: hot southern vegetables, like peppers and courgettes, with olives, Bayonne ham and scrambled eggs. Sometimes it is a chunkier dish, made with halved very softly boiled eggs, the yolks of which melt into the vegetables.

Of course, being me, I couldn't just adopt such a dish for my menu. My brain began churning over ways to take the essence of the dish and present it in a new way. Instead of eggs I substituted rice for one dish, pasta for another. To take my family tree of dishes even further, I began experimenting with pipérade risotto as a stuffing for chicken or rabbit legs, both of which regularly appear on my menus.

Classic Pipérade

Pipérade in its traditional form is a great dish for a brunch or light lunch. This is how I would make it...

serves 4

4 warm soft-boiled eggs, halved

for the Pipérade Vegetables:

100 ml olive oil

1 large courgette, sliced at an angle

1 medium aubergine, sliced at an angle and then each slice halved

12 small shallots, peeled

8 baby fennel, trimmed

2 red peppers, deseeded and cut into large strips

2 yellow peppers, deseeded and cut into large strips

1 head of garlic, cloves separated and peeled

100 ml Sun-dried Tomato Juice (page 12)

freshly ground salt and black pepper

good handful of black olives

20 basil leaves

handful of mixed fresh herbs, to serve

1 Prepare the Pipérade Vegetables: heat the olive oil in a pan, add the vegetables, garlic and sun-dried tomato juice and season. Cover with a tight-fitting lid and leave over a low heat until the vegetables are just soft to the touch.

2 Remove the vegetables from the heat and add the olives and basil to warm through.

3 Carefully arrange the vegetables on 4 plates with the soft-boiled eggs and serve garnished with fresh herbs.

Penne with Pipérade and Mozzarella

serves 4

400 g penne

a little olive oil

2 large tomatoes

100 ml Sun-dried Tomato Juice (page 12)

25 g butter

25 g tapenade

20 small cherry tomatoes

100 g mozzarella, diced

Pipérade Vegetables (as above)

salt and pepper

10 basil leaves, chopped

for the garnish:

fresh herbs, such as basil and chervil

shavings of fresh Parmesan cheese (made using a swivel peeler)

1 Cook the penne in boiling salted water with a spoonful of olive oil until just al dente. Drain and reserve.

2 Briefly blanch the large tomatoes in boiling water, refresh in cold water, then remove the skins. Quarter them, scrape out the seeds and dice the flesh into ½-cm cubes.

3 Put the sun-dried tomato juice in a pan and bubble up until reduced to a syrup.

4 Melt the butter in a pan and add the tomato syrup and tapenade, and heat through.

5 Add the pasta and stir around until the butter coats it.

6 Add the cherry tomatoes, mozzarella and pipérade vegetables.

7 Stir until the vegetables have warmed through and the cheese has melted and coated the pasta. Season.

8 Stir in the diced tomatoes and basil.

9 Serve garnished with herbs and Parmesan shavings.

Pipérade Risotto with Red Pepper Reduction

serves 4

a little olive oil

5 shallots, finely diced

350 g risotto rice

5 tbsp white wine

600 ml hot vegetable stock

300 ml Sun-dried Tomato Juice (page 12)

½ tbsp tapenade

250 g mascarpone cheese

40 g grated Parmesan cheese

50 g shredded basil

Pipérade Vegetables (page 122)

for the garnish:

a little Red Pepper Reduction (page 12)

dash of truffle oil

4 slices of Dried Aubergine (page 15)

4 slices of Dried Tomato (page 15)

strips of Parmesan Crackling (page 118)

fresh mixed herbs, such as basil sprigs and red shiso

1 Heat the oil in a pan, add the shallots and sweat gently until translucent.

2 Add the rice and stir to coat.

3 Add the white wine, stirring all the time, until the wine is absorbed.

4 Gradually add the hot vegetable stock, a ladleful at a time. Make sure you stir well after each addition and continue to stir, until the liquid is entirely absorbed by the rice.

5 Add the sun-dried tomato juice and continue to cook until this is also absorbed and the rice is soft.

6 Stir in the tapenade, mascarpone, Parmesan and basil.

7 To serve: arrange the risotto on plates, top with pipérade vegetables, then drizzle around the red pepper reduction and truffle oil, and garnish with dried aubergine and tomato, Parmesan Crackling and the herbs.

Some people say that you shouldn't wash mushrooms — the point is that you shouldn't let them soak up water. Mushrooms are about 75 per cent water and if you wash them and leave them damp they just soak up the excess like a sponge. Then, just like scallops, they will let this moisture out when you pan-fry them.

If you clean the mushrooms well with a small brush, then put them under running water just before you cook them, drain them and dry them well, they should be fine.

When you pan-fry different types of wild mushroom, start with the biggest and toughest, then gradually add the smaller finer ones, finishing if you like with the Japanese enoki, lovely tiny white caps with long stems, which take only around 10 seconds to cook.

Wild Mushrooms in Crêpes

In the north of France, where I was brought up, we have a local dish of mushrooms in mornay sauce wrapped in a pancake. When I began cooking at The Provence Restaurant in Lymington, close to the New Forest, with its natural treasure of wild mushrooms, I began to elaborate on the idea.

I would go out at dawn during the mushroom season, armed with baskets and tripping over roots and brambles in the half-light, searching for ceps, chanterelles, etc., then I would bring them back to the kitchen and experiment with new ideas.

The first recipe given here is for a simple dish of wild mushrooms wrapped in crêpes. The second, which appears on my restaurant menus, is a result of those early-morning cooking sessions: a richer, more elegant variation on the same theme, made with chicken mousse and served with both a mushroom and a port sauce.

serves 4

for the crêpes:

110 g flour

300 ml milk

1 whole egg, plus 1 extra yolk, beaten

1 tbsp sunflower or other flavourless oil

pinch of salt and pepper

handful of poppy seeds

olive oil

for the mushroom mixture:

1 kg mixed field and wild mushrooms, stems removed and reserved

a little olive oil

10 g shallots, chopped

1 garlic clove, chopped

25 g basil, chopped

20 g tarragon, chopped

10 g chives, chopped

freshly ground salt and black pepper

1 First make the crêpes: sift the seasoned flour into a bowl. Make a well in the centre and add the milk, egg and oil. Gradually incorporate until smooth. Stir in the poppy seeds.

2 Heat a crêpe pan, then pour in a thin film of oil. When that is hot, pour a thin circle of crêpe mixture into the centre of the pan and swirl so that the mixture spreads over the entire surface. Cook briefly until the underside is golden when you lift up a corner. Flip over and cook until the second side is golden. Slide on to a plate and keep warm. Cook 3 more in the same way. (Any leftover batter will keep in the fridge for 2–3 days.)

3 Prepare the mushroom mixture: clean and remove the stalks from the mushrooms and then slice the mushrooms.

4 Heat a little olive oil in a pan and sweat the shallots and garlic gently until softened. Then turn up the heat and add the mushrooms with half the herbs. Sauté briefly and season. Drain in a colander. Put the drained mushrooms in a bowl with the remaining herbs and mix well. Keep warm.

5 Pile some mushroom mix on each pancake and roll up or fold as you wish.

Steamed Wild Mushroom Gâteau with Crêpes, Port Sauce, Porcini Oil and Parmesan Crackling

serves 4

4 crêpes (see previous pages)
Mushroom Mixture (see previous pages)

for the Chicken Mousse
250 g chicken breast
freshly ground salt and pepper
1 egg
500 ml double cream

for the Mushroom Sauce:
a little olive oil
100 g shallots, finely chopped
2 garlic cloves, finely chopped
100 g celery, finely chopped
50 g mixed herbs, such as thyme and rosemary
1 litre chicken stock
300 ml double cream
100 g preserved foie gras, diced
15 g butter, cut into cubes

for the Port Sauce:
a little oil
100 g shallots, finely chopped
2 garlic cloves, finely chopped
100 g celery, finely chopped
1 sprig of thyme
1 bay leaf
200 ml port
100 ml Madeira
100 ml veal stock

15 g butter, cut into cubes, plus more for
greasing the ramekins

for the garnish:
a little olive oil
handful of wild mushrooms
cep (porcini) oil
Parmesan Crackling (page 118)
sprigs of chervil

1 Make the crêpes and prepare the mushroom
mixture as on the previous pages, reserving the
stalks and drained juice for the sauce.
2 Make the chicken mousse: trim the chicken
of all fat and skin. Chop and season. Put into a
food processor and blend to a paste. Add the
egg and blend again for 10 seconds. Scrape all
the mixture down the sides of the mixing bowl
with a spatula, and incorporate. Add the cream
very slowly, turning the machine off every few
seconds to mix again with the spatula, until
everything is well incorporated. Put through a
fine sieve.
3 Add the chicken mousse to the bowl
containing the mushroom mixture.
4 Place each crêpe in a buttered and seasoned
ramekin, so that the crêpe overhangs the
edges. Fill with the mushroom mixture, then
fold the overlapping edges of the crêpe
over the top to enclose the filling completely.
Wrap each ramekin with cling-film, put in a
steamer and steam for 30 minutes.

5 Meanwhile make the mushroom sauce: heat a
little olive oil in a pan and sauté the shallots,
garlic, celery, finely chopped mushroom stalks
and herbs, until the shallots are softened.
6 Add the chicken stock and reserved
mushroom juice and bubble up until reduced
by three-quarters.
7 Add the cream and reduce again by half.
8 Put through a fine sieve into a clean pan,
stir in the foie gras and wave in the butter.
Keep warm.
9 Make the port sauce: heat a little olive oil in
a pan and sauté the shallots, garlic, celery and
herbs.
10 Add the port and Madeira and bubble up
until reduced by three-quarters.
11 Add the stock and reduce again until the
sauce coats the back of a spoon.
12 Put through a fine sieve into a clean pan,
and wave in the butter.
13 Prepare the garnish: heat a little oil in a
pan and quickly sauté the wild mushrooms.
14 Place a steamed mushroom gâteau in the
centre of each plate, and scatter the mushroom
mixture around and on top. Pour a little of
each sauce around the plate. Drizzle on a little
cep oil and garnish with Parmesan Crackling
and chervil.

carrots

Carrots are such humble things and yet, if you buy them carefully, you can extract so much flavour from them and with a little imagination you can construct something very delicate and impressive. Look for small, brightly coloured carrots that are not at all woody.

Steamed Lettuce and Carrot Gâteau with Hollandaise

This is a simpler version of the restaurant dish that follows. In this you just make a purée of carrots, herbs, garlic, Emmental cheese and cream, and steam it in moulds lined with blanched lettuce. In the second recipe you enhance the purée with some carrots which have been caramelized in honey and olive oil, and garnish the dish with baby carrots coated with Orange and Cardamom Reduction.

serves 4

2 Cos lettuces
freshly ground salt and black pepper
425 g carrots, chopped
25 g basil, chopped
15 g tarragon, chopped
3 garlic cloves, chopped
3 tbsp double cream
75 g Emmental cheese, grated
3 eggs
butter for greasing the moulds
Hollandaise Sauce (page 46)

1 Select enough large lettuce leaves to line 4 dariole moulds or heatproof cups. Dip these for a second in boiling salted water, drain and refresh in cold water, drain again and reserve.

2 Cook the carrots in boiling salted water until just tender and drain.

3 Put these in a blender with the herbs and garlic and 1 tablespoon of the double cream and blitz until you have a smooth purée.

4 Add the grated Emmental and season well.

5 Mix the eggs and the remaining cream together, then add to the carrot mixture.

6 Grease the dariole moulds or heatproof cups with a little butter, then line with the blanched lettuce leaves.

7 Spoon in the carrot mixture, then cover with cling-film.

8 Place in a steamer and steam for about 30 minutes or until the mixture has set.

9 Meanwhile make the Hollandaise Sauce as described on page 46.

10 Remove the dariole moulds or cups from the steamer, carefully take off the cling-film and turn out a carrot gâteau on each plate.

11 Serve with the Hollandaise.

Steamed Lettuce and Caramelized Carrot Gâteau

serves 4

2 Cos lettuces
500 g carrots
freshly ground salt and black pepper
1 tbsp olive oil
1 tbsp clear honey
25 g basil, chopped
15 g tarragon, chopped
3 garlic cloves, chopped
5 tbsp double cream
200 g Emmental cheese

3 eggs
a little butter
Hollandaise Sauce (page 46)

for the garnish:

12 baby carrots
2 tbsp Orange and Cardamom Reduction
   (page 11, reserving the cardamom pods)
Basil Oil (page 11)
sprigs of chervil
chives

1 Keep any small lettuce leaves back for garnish, then blanch enough large ones to line 4 dariole moulds or heatproof cups as opposite.

2 Cook the baby carrots for the garnish in boiling salted water until just tender. Reserve.

3 Cut half of the ordinary carrots into cubes of about 1 cm. Sprinkle with salt, put into a steamer and steam for about 8 minutes or until just al dente.

4 Meanwhile, chop the remaining carrots and cook in boiling salted water until just tender.

5 Put the olive oil and honey in a pan over a low heat, add the steamed carrots, herbs and garlic and toss well to coat. Cook until the carrots are soft and sticky. Remove the pan from the heat.

6 Drain the boiled carrots, then purée them with 1 tablespoon of the double cream. Add this mixture to the honeyed carrots and, while still warm, mix in the grated Emmental. Season well.

7 Mix the eggs and the remaining cream together, then add to the carrot mixture.

8 Grease 4 dariole moulds or heatproof cups with a little butter, then line with the blanched large lettuce leaves.

9 Spoon in the carrot mixture, then cover with cling-film.

10 Place in a steamer and steam for about 30 minutes, or until the mixture has set.

11 Meanwhile make the Hollandaise Sauce as described on page 46.

12 Finish preparing the garnish: heat the orange and cardamom reduction in a pan, add the reserved baby carrots and toss well until they are coated.

13 Remove the dariole moulds or cups from the steamer, carefully take off the cling-film and turn out a carrot gâteau on each plate.

14 Remove the baby carrots from the orange and cardamom reduction, reserving this, and arrange three on top of each gâteau. Serve with a little Hollandaise Sauce, drizzle around some basil oil and the remaining orange and cardamom reduction, and garnish with the cardamom pods, small lettuce leaves, chervil and chives.

rts

The pâtisserie
in my kitchens sums up my
attitude to cooking, because there is
such scope for having fun with classical
recipes. Although you can decorate according
to your mood, however, the basic recipes
require careful measuring of ingredients, more
so than in any other section of the kitchen.
My safe pair of hands in this respect is
Duncan Impey, the Novelli Group pastry chef,
and another of the Four Seasons brigade. My
love affair with pastry began as a teenager,
when I learned to temper chocolate at the
local pâtisserie, to get that wonderful
gloss and sheen. One Easter I won the
competition for the best creation, with
a cathedral made out of chocolate and
icing, which was displayed in the shop.
Unfortunately, an old lady dropped
something on it and smashed its roof
before my parents could even see it,
but it didn't matter... making it
had made me realize that it was in
my blood to be creative with
food, especially desserts.

Some of the best ideas in cooking happen by accident. The idea of a tart cooked upside down, with the fruit underneath the pastry, then turned the right way up, was made famous by the Tatin sisters, who ran a restaurant in Lamotte-Beuvron, near Orléans, at the turn of the century. One story is that they were in a hurry and, instead of making a classic apple tart with crème pâtissière, they simply put the sugared apple into the tart tin and covered it with pastry. When it was baked and they then flipped it over, they discovered the wonderful caramelized surface of the apples, which has given the dish its endless appeal.

My grandmother used to make enormous tartes tatins in great big pans with handles. When she turned them over the fruit would fly out everywhere. Take it from me, it is much easier to handle small individual ones, as we do in the restaurant!

The classic tarte tatin is made with halved apples covered with pastry. We sometimes make one with a whole Pink Golden Delicious apple, peeled and cored. These days, though, most chefs make a more elegant tart with apples cut into quarters, arranged in a circular pattern. Granny Smith apples are best as they hold their texture and flavour.

A perfect tarte tatin has a combination of crisp pastry, firm but properly cooked fruit, and crunchy caramel. Traditionally, the fruit is caramelized by putting butter and sugar into the tatin pan then adding the apples, covering them with puff pastry and starting the cooking process on the hob. When the butter and sugar begin to bubble and turn golden, the pan is transferred to the oven.

I prefer to make the caramel separately, then pour it into tatin tins lined with baking paper, before arranging the fruit. This gives a dark crunchy, mirror-like caramel glaze to the fruit, while the baking paper stops the caramel from sticking to the pan, and makes it easier to turn out the tarte.

We have a whole repertoire of tatins, made with different fruits, even banana and strawberry, which you might think are impossible to make without the fruit turning to purée! When we created the recipes, we first put the fruit in the oven without the pastry to see how long we would need to cook them without their disintegrating. Then we experimented with the pastry, rolled out to different thicknesses, until we found the cooking times to match.

Apple Tarte Tatin

makes 4 individual tartes

50 g unsalted butter, cut into cubes, plus more for greasing
4 sheets of ready-made puff pastry
6 Granny Smith apples
100 g caster sugar
icing sugar, for dusting

to serve:
Vanilla or Caramel Ice-cream (page 150, 152)
Caramel Springs (page 17)

1 Line the base of 4 individual 10-cm round tatin pans or 10-cm baking tins with rounds of baking paper. Grease the papers with a little butter.
2 Roll the puff pastry out into circles about 10 cm in diameter and 2 mm thick.
3 Peel the apples, core them and cut them into quarters.
4 Heat the caster sugar with 2 tablespoons of water in a heavy-based saucepan and cook very gently until the caramel is light gold.
5 Remove from the heat and add the cubed butter, stirring well until it is completely incorporated.
6 Pour a thin layer of caramel on the base of each lined tatin pan or tin. Pack the apple quarters in a circular pattern on top of the caramel.
7 Drape a circle of pastry over the top, then tuck it in well to completely encase the apple. Leave to rest in a cool place for 20 minutes, so that the pastry won't shrink when it goes in the oven.
8 Preheat the oven to 230°C/450°F/gas 8. Dust each circle of pastry with a little icing sugar, put in the preheated oven and bake for 18-20 minutes, or until the pastry is golden brown and the apples soft.

9 Remove the tarts from the oven and leave to rest for 1 minute to let the caramel cool and set slightly.
10 Remember hot caramel burns the skin badly, so please be careful when you turn out your tarts. To do so, place a dessert plate over the top of each pan and, with a twist of the wrist, very carefully flip pan and plate over together, so that the tart ends up, apple-side upwards, on the plate. Remove the paper.
11 Serve, if you like, with a scoop of vanilla or caramel ice-cream on top and some caramel springs. Dust the whole plate with icing sugar.

Banana Tatin

Banana tatin is the brainchild of Filip Tibos and Mike Ouchbakou, who were my talented pastry chefs at The Four Seasons. When we were frantically busy in the kitchen, I used to keep going by eating bananas, which I pinched from them. One day they presented me with a banana tarte tatin. It was a very daring thing to try, because banana turns to pulp so quickly when it is cooked. I had never liked cooked banana up to that point, but I loved it straight away. The important thing is to use very firm bananas.

Follow the recipe for Apple Tatin on the previous pages, but roll the pastry out into thinner circles (about 1.5 mm) and, instead of apples, slice 6 bananas into cylinders about 2.5 cm in length. Pack these upright on top of the caramel with one in the centre and the rest around, like petals. Bake at 220°C/425°F/gas 7 for 15 minutes.

Serve, if you like, with Rum and Raisin Ice-cream (page 150), and decorate with Banana Crisp (below).

Banana Crisp

To make enough to decorate 4 desserts: preheat the oven to 110°C/230°F/gas ¼. In a food processor, blitz 1 banana to a smooth purée, then mix in the juice of ¼ lemon and ½ tablespoon of icing sugar. Spread the mixture thinly over a non-stick baking tray and put in the oven for about 3 hours, until the mixture is completely dried out.

Remove the tray from the oven and, while the banana mixture is still warm, ease it out gently with a spatula. Leave flat on a clean work surface until cool and crisp, then break into pieces and use as you like.

Strawberry Tatin

Make as for Banana Tatin, but use large, very firm strawberries and bake for 20 minutes. Serve, if you like, with Vanilla Ice-cream (page 150).

Fig Tatin

Around May, we are able to get deep purple French figs, which are firm, yet ripe and fruity, just right for tarte tatin. At other times of the year we use green figs, which must be cooked for longer to bring out their sweetness. Make the fig tatin as the Strawberry Tatin above, substituting 3 whole figs for the strawberries. If using purple French figs, bake for about 15–20 minutes; for green figs, bake for about 25 minutes. Serve, if you like, with Caramel Ice-cream (page 152).

Pineapple Tatin

Make as for Apple Tatin (previous pages), substituting a ring of fresh pineapple, cut to about 1.5 cm thick, for the apples, and poach the rings first in stock syrup (page 157) for about 15 minutes. Serve, if you like, with Coconut Ice-cream (page 150).

crème brûlée

The secret of a good crème brûlée is in the making of the custard, which must be absolutely smooth. When you boil the cream and milk you need patience to let it come to the boil very slowly. Then, when you add the cream and milk to your egg yolks and sugar, again you must do it very slowly and gently, whipping all the time, otherwise you will end up with something that resembles scrambled eggs.

When the brûlées are ready to come out of the oven, they should be set, but still wobble like a jelly. Once they hit the cool air, they will become more solid. If you leave them any longer in the oven, they will become too stodgy when cool.

Some people like a thick brûlée crust on a crème brûlée, but I think it should be a thin surface which will crack sharply when you break it with a spoon. We glaze vanilla or mandarin brûlée with unrefined caster sugar, which forms a glassy, brittle surface. For the richer-flavoured brûlées, like coconut or almond, we use demerara sugar, which has a slightly softer and more crunchy texture.

Vanilla Crème Brûlée

serves 4

240 ml double cream
½ vanilla pod, split
160 ml milk
7 egg yolks
80 g unrefined caster sugar, plus a little extra
    for glazing

1 Preheat the oven to 110°C/230°F/gas ¼.
2 In a pan, bring the cream, vanilla pod and milk to the boil. Remove the pan from the heat and allow to cool slightly.
3 In a bowl, mix together the egg yolks and sugar.
4 Add the hot cream-and-milk mixture to the bowl slowly, mixing well. Pour through a fine sieve into four deep 6-cm ramekin dishes.
5 Cook in the preheated oven for 50–60 minutes, until the surface is just firm but the brûlées are still a little wobbly (check each one at regular intervals, and remove as necessary).
6 Leave to cool, then chill for 2–3 hours.
7 Sprinkle sugar all over the top, then tip the ramekins and tap the sides gently to let the excess sugar fall off, leaving a thin film of sugar on the top.
8 Either put under a preheated grill or use a blow-torch to caramelize the sugar. As the sugar melts, tilt the ramekins slightly to spread it all over the surface. You should end up with a thin golden layer, which will crisp up as it cools down.

Coconut Crème Brûlée

Make as for Vanilla Crème Brûlée, but use 280 ml double cream, 80 ml coconut milk, 1 tablespoon Malibu, 6 egg yolks and 60 g caster sugar, and sprinkle on unrefined demerara sugar, rather than caster sugar, for the glaze.

'Smooth custard
beneath a glassy,
brittle surface.'

Mandarin Brûlée

Making a citrus fruit brûlée requires a little care, as the acidity of the
fruit doesn't naturally mix with milk. We reduce the mandarin juice with
sugar to a thick syrup first, before combining it with the milk and cream.

serves 4

500 ml mandarin juice (about 15 mandarins),
 plus grated zest of 3 mandarins
130 g unrefined caster sugar, plus a little for
 glazing
240 ml double cream
160 ml milk
¼ vanilla pod, split
7 egg yolks

for decoration (optional)
4 Tuile Cigars (page 143)
8 Caramel Springs (page 17)

the day before:

1 If decorating with tuile cigars, make these in advance.

2 Put the mandarin juice and zest in a pan with 50g of the sugar, bring to the boil, then turn the
heat down and simmer until reduced down to around 1 teaspoon of thick syrup.

3 Put the cream, milk and mandarin syrup in a pan with the vanilla pod, scraping in the seeds,
and bring to the boil. Remove the pan from the heat and allow to cool.

4 In a bowl, mix together the egg yolks and remaining sugar. Add the cream and milk mixture
slowly, mixing well. Leave to cool, then put in the fridge overnight, so that the flavours infuse.

next day:

5 Preheat the oven to 110°C/230°F/gas ¼. Pour the brûlée mixture through a fine sieve into 4
ramekin dishes and proceed as for Vanilla Crème Brûlée (opposite).

6 If decorating with tuile cigars, insert them into each caramelized top as soon as you remove it
from under the grill or have finished using the blow-torch, while the caramel is still soft. As it sets
hard it will keep the cigar in place. Decorate with Caramel Springs.

tiramisu

By adding gelatine to this classic Italian dessert you can transform it from the soft cream usually served in a glass into something free-standing and elegant.

serves 6

1 genoese sponge
3 egg yolks
100 g unrefined caster sugar
250 g mascarpone cheese
250 ml double cream
2 leaves of gelatine, soaked in cold water for
    5 minutes
1 small cup of espresso or strong coffee
2 tbsp Kahlúa

for decoration:
a little cocoa powder
White Chocolate Sauce (optional, page 152)
Dark Chocolate Sauce (optional, page 152)

1 Using a 6-cm ring mould as a cutter, cut 4 discs from the sponge.

2 In a bowl, whisk the egg yolks and sugar until pale. Add the mascarpone and mix well.

3 Whip the double cream until it just begins to thicken, then add this to the mixture.

4 Transfer 2 tablespoons of the mixture to a pan and heat gently. Squeeze excess liquid out of the soaking gelatine, add to the pan and stir until dissolved, then add to the rest of the cream, mixing well.

5 Mix the coffee and Kahlúa in a bowl. Dip the sponge discs briefly in this mixture, then put them in the base of 4 deep 6-cm ring moulds.

6 Pour in enough mascarpone mixture to come to the top of each mould and chill in the fridge for about 2½ hours until set.

7 Dust the top of each tiramisu with cocoa powder, carefully slide the cutter moulds off and serve, if you like, with a mixture of white and dark chocolate sauces.

Tiramisu Boat with Three Sauces

In a flight of fantasy for the restaurants we partner the simple tiramisu with tuile, caramel and dessert sauces, to make an extravagant model boat!

serves 6

6 individual Tiramisu (see above)
1 recipe quantity Tuile mixture (page 143)
cocoa powder, for colouring
Caramel (page 17)
6 Caramel Springs (page 17)
Crème Anglaise (page 153)
Coffee Sauce (page 153)
Dark Chocolate Sauce (page 152)

1 Make the tiramisu as above and keep in the fridge until ready to serve (do not dust with cocoa powder until the last minute).

2 Make up the tuile mixture, including some with cocoa powder for piping (see page 143).

3 Preheat the oven to 180°C/350°F/gas 4. To make the boat, make some stencils as follows: take one sheet of card and cut out 4 long petal shapes. These will form the base of each boat. Spread some tuile mixture over the top and carefully remove the card. With your chocolate mixture, pipe a line all the way around each petal shape, a little in from the edge of the tuile.

4 Bake for about 4 minutes until the tuile is just beginning to colour.

5 Remove from the oven and, while still warm, bend the ends of each boat upwards slightly. Leave to cool.

6 Take another sheet of card and cut out 5 squares, approximately 6 cm. This is enough for the sails for one boat. Spread the mixture over the card, then remove it carefully and pipe an edging around the sails with chocolate tuile. Then, with a skewer, make a hole towards the centre-top and bottom of each sail (the rigging will be threaded through here, see picture). Bake as above.

7 When the mixture comes out of the oven and while still warm, drape it over the length of a rolling pin to curve the sails. Leave to cool.

8 Repeat until you have five sails for each boat. If you have enough baking sheets you can make them all at once, rather than in batches, but it may then be difficult to mould all the sails while they are still warm; in that case just put them back in the oven briefly until they are pliable again.

9 To make the caramel masts, trail some caramel up and down over some greaseproof paper. You need enough to make three masts per boat. Leave the caramel to harden, then snap into equal lengths.

10 Remove the tiramisu from the fridge and dust the top of each one with cocoa powder. Place a 'boat' in the centre of each of 6 plates, then place a tiramisu in the centre of each boat.

11 Insert 3 caramel masts into each tiramisu, one vertical, the others pointing forwards and backwards at angles. Thread 2 sails on to the back and centre masts, using the holes in the tuile. Thread one sail on to the front. Slide a caramel spring over the end of each mast.

12 Make a sea around each boat by pouring on a little of each sauce, then run the handle of a spoon through them to create a wave pattern.

tuiles

There is nothing new about tuile. It is a classic biscuit mix that has been used over the years to accompany all kinds of desserts. What is exciting is how you work with it as, while it is warm, it can be fashioned into whatever shape you like. If you prefer, you can use a food processor to make the mixture.

Tuile Biscuits

makes about 24

100 g unsalted butter
100 g icing sugar
½ tbsp vanilla extract
whites of 3 eggs
100 g flour

1 Preheat the oven to 200°C/400°F/gas 6.
2 In a bowl, cream the butter, sugar and vanilla extract together. Gradually beat in the egg white, then fold in the flour until you have a smooth paste. Chill for about 2 hours.
3 Place small spoonfuls of the mixture about 10 cm apart on a non-stick baking sheet, then spread these out with a spatula into rounds.
4 Bake for about 4 minutes until the mixture is just beginning to colour (keep checking).

5 Remove from the oven and leave to cool very slightly until you can handle them. Shape the rounds by draping them over the length of a rolling pin or as described below. Leave until completely cool and set, then lift off gently. You can keep the tuiles in an airtight container for up to a week.

Other Shapes:

Baskets

Depending on the size you want, drape your warm rounds of baked tuile over the top of a clean bottle or gently press them inside a tea cup or dariole mould and leave until cool.

Stencils

Take a piece of clean card and cut out the shapes you want: i.e. flowers or leaves. Lay the card on your baking tray and spread the mixture over the top. Lift the card off carefully before putting the mixture into the oven.

Cigars

Take a piece of clean card and cut out a series of oblongs about 1 cm wide and 20 cm long. Proceed as for the stencils above. When the tuile comes out of the oven and is cool enough to handle, wind each strip loosely around a sharpening steel or wooden spoon. Leave until cold, then slide off.

Chocolate Edging

The tuile shapes can be decorated by mixing a little of the tuile mixture with a little cocoa powder. This can be piped around the edges of flower shapes, or along the centre of the strips for 'cigars' before the tuile goes into the oven.

When I was a child, before I went to bed at night I used to eat a piece of pure dark chocolate to help calm me down. Then, as now, I found it difficult to sleep, because my mind would always be racing, full of ideas and plans. My mother found that the best chocolate, made with 70% cocoa solids and no added sugar, can have a relaxing effect.

Chocolate Marquise

This is a classic dessert that can be served simply on its own, or with a little white chocolate sauce, cream or crème anglaise and a dusting of icing sugar and/or cocoa powder. However, we use it as a base for one of the dishes that seems to have earned me the most publicity, the Jack-in-the-box.

serves 6

six 6-cm diameter rounds of light sponge cake about
    5 mm thick (you can buy ready-made sponge and cut it
    to shape or make your own Genoese sponge)
a little brandy
115 g good-quality dark bitter chocolate
whites of 5 eggs
50 g caster sugar
300 ml double cream, lightly whipped until standing in
    soft peaks

for decoration:
halved strawberries
tiny mint sprigs
icing sugar
cocoa powder

1 Brush the rounds of sponge lightly with a little brandy and place one in the bottom of each of six 6-cm round moulds.
2 Break the chocolate into squares and put these in a bowl. Place this bowl over a pan of hot water set over a very low heat and let the chocolate melt, stirring constantly. Do not let the chocolate boil or its flavour and texture will be impaired.
3 In another bowl, whisk the egg whites until they form soft peaks. Fold the sugar into the egg whites, then fold in the whipped cream. Fold this mixture into the chocolate.
4 Spoon the resulting chocolate mousse into the moulds and put them into the fridge to set, about 2 hours.
5 When ready to serve, run a warmed knife around the outside of each of the moulds and then invert them to turn out the marquises on 6 serving plates. Decorate with strawberry halves and mint sprigs, then dust lightly with icing sugar and cocoa powder.

Jack-in-the-box

The first time I made the Jack-in-the-box was the best. Sometimes, like scoring a perfect goal in football, everything comes together at the right time and you achieve something quite special which can never be reproduced in quite the same way. The idea obviously came from the child's toy, which I wanted to recreate with food; but, unlike wood and fabric of course, food is perishable. Changes in temperature, movement, heat and the weight of the garnishes destroy it minute by minute from the moment it is made.

That first Jack-in-the-box was made spontaneously, but then came the nightmare of trying to teach the other chefs in my kitchen at The Provence Restaurant to copy it quickly and in large quantities, without someone having to go out and tell the customers, 'Sorry you will have to wait 20 minutes, because the chef is cracking up trying to get the caramel right!'

When you are not in a pressurized kitchen, though, it is a fun dessert to make. One day, when you have the time and you are feeling creative, why not have a go? The caramel 'sides' to the box can be made in advance and stored in an airtight container.

serves 4

4 Chocolate Marquise, as opposite

neutral oil, such as sunflower, for greasing
575 g caster sugar
2 tablespoons liquid glucose
4 tablespoons ground almonds

for decoration:
100 g roasted hazelnuts
3 tbsp icing sugar
16 Caramel Springs (page 17)

1 Make the chocolate marquise as described opposite, but in 6-cm square moulds, and chill.

2 Preheat the oven to 180°C/350°F/gas 4.

3 To make the sides of the box: lay out a sheet of greaseproof paper on a work surface and oil it lightly.

4 Put the sugar and glucose in a heavy-based pan and heat gently until a golden caramel forms. Remove from the heat and carefully pour the caramel over the oiled greaseproof paper.

5 Leave to cool until brittle, then smash two-thirds into little pieces with a rolling pin. Put the caramel pieces in a blender with the ground almonds and process to a powder with the consistency of caster sugar.

6 Have ready a large non-stick baking tray. Sprinkle the powdered caramel very thinly over the baking tray to an even layer covering an area of 36 x 30 cm. Put the tray in the preheated oven for about 3 minutes. Keep checking it and remove the moment the caramel has melted again and resembles a sheet of glass.

7 Leave to cool for literally 1 minute then, using a clean ruler and a sharp knife, score it across in a grid of lines 6 cm apart horizontally and vertically, forming 30 squares. You will actually only need 24 of these squares, but the extras allow for the possibility of any splintering or otherwise getting damaged. Score 10 of the squares in half again into 2 equal rectangles. When the caramel is completely cold, snap along the scored lines to break the caramel into squares, plus the 20 rectangles (again, you will only need

16 rectangles, the others are extras).

8 Put the reserved caramel into a pan and melt it gently. You will use this as glue and glaze for assembling the box and for coating the hazelnuts. Remove the chocolate marquises from the fridge. Turn each out of its mould as described above and place each one in the centre of a large plate.

9 As you work with the caramel, constantly dust your fingers with icing sugar, to keep the caramel from sticking to them. Stick a square of caramel on each side of each marquise (these should cling to the chocolate), then 'weld' the corners together, using a hot knife.

10 Take 4 of the rectangles, dip one long edge of each into the warmed caramel and stick one to the top of each 'side' of the box, to resemble an open lid. Repeat with the remaining boxes.

11 Dip the hazelnuts into the caramel and pile them into the top of each box.

12 Very carefully position the springs to look as though they are popping out of the top of the box. Dust the whole thing with icing sugar — and pour yourself a large brandy!

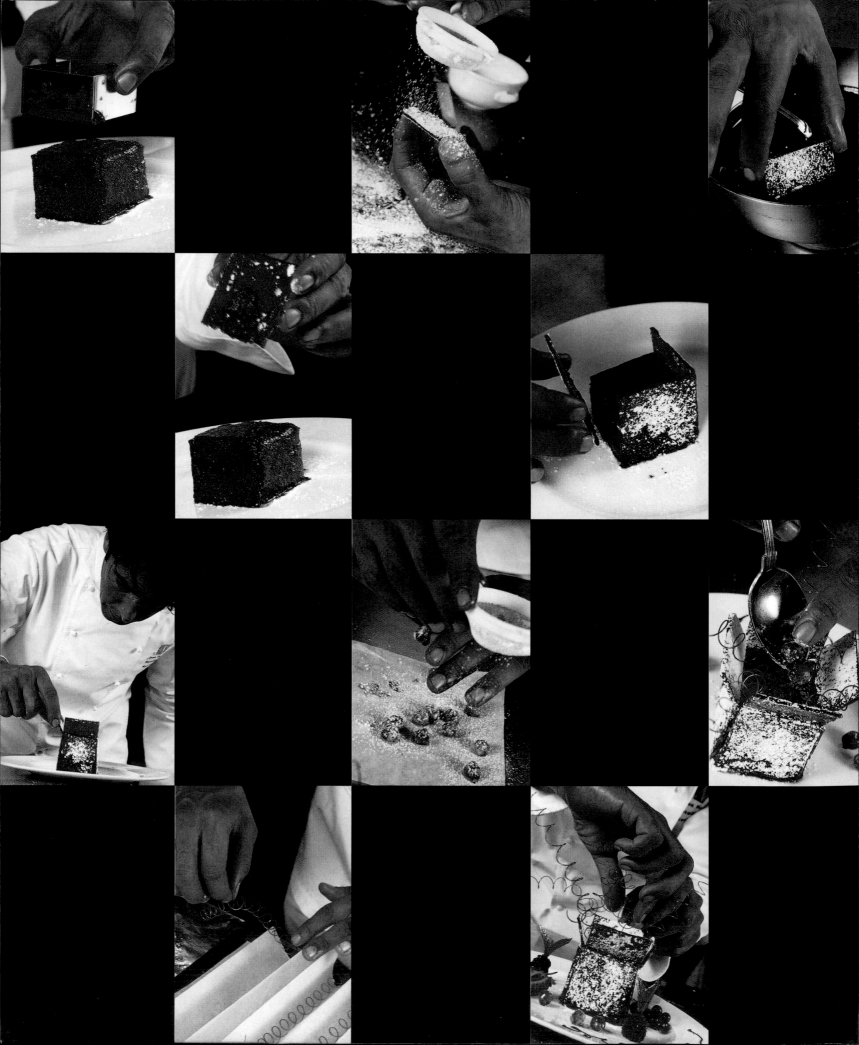

Chocolate Pudding

Most chefs have a version of a chocolate pudding that is firm on the outside, but when cut open reveals a soft, silky chocolate centre. There are many tricks to help achieve this effect, but this is one of the simplest. All that is required is to bake the pudding to a precise timing which allows the outside of the puddings to become firm, leaving the centre soft.

When we cook this dessert it is the only time we have an alarm clock in the kitchen. When the puddings are ready they will rise up in the middle and feel firm to the touch. Don't leave them in any longer as once they begin to crack, it means the centre will start to firm up too, ruining the whole point of the dessert.

serves 6

250 g unsalted butter, plus a little extra for greasing moulds

5 eggs, plus 5 extra yolks

125 g unrefined caster sugar

250 g bitter dark chocolate (70% cocoa solids), broken up

50 g plain flour, sifted

the day before:

1 In a bowl, beat together the eggs, egg yolks and sugar until pale.

2 Meanwhile, melt the chocolate and butter gently in a bowl set over a pan of hot water. Remove from the heat. Slowly add to the egg mixture, beating until smooth. Fold in the flour.

3 Pour into buttered moulds before it begins to firm up. Chill overnight.

next day:

4 Preheat the oven to 180°C/350°F/gas 4. Bake for about 10-15 minutes until the centres dome and feel dry (checking regularly).

5 Turn out and serve.

Hot and Cold and White Chocolate Plate

serves 6

Tuile mixture (see page 143)

White Chocolate Sauce (page 152)

Dark Chocolate Sauce (page 152)

6 Chocolate Puddings (as above)

White Chocolate Ice-cream (page 150)

6 Caramel Springs (page 17)

6 sprigs of redcurrants

icing sugar

6 sprigs of mint

flat block of dark chocolate

1 Make 6 tuile biscuits in the shapes of spoons with tapering handles, using stencils, as shown on page 143. While still warm, bend the spoon 'handles' (see picture opposite).

2 Drizzle the chocolate sauces in zig-zags across the serving plates. Place a chocolate pudding off centre and a tuile spoon alongside. Place a scoop of white chocolate ice-cream on the tuile spoon. Decorate with the caramel springs.

3 Decorate with some redcurrants dusted with icing sugar, a sprig of mint and some chocolate curls made by shaving strips off a block of chocolate with a vegetable peeler. These can be left loose or wound into cigar shapes to make a receptacle for the caramel springs.

ice-creams, sorbets & sweet sauces

Everyone I know — from children to grandparents — loves ice-cream. There is something very sensual about the smoothest, creamiest ice-cream that makes it a perfect medium for experimenting with intense flavours. And it can be what you want it to be: a scoop in a cornet on a hot day or one element in a dramatic dessert.

Vanilla Ice-cream

serves 4

3 egg yolks
75 g unrefined caster sugar
300 ml milk
150 ml double cream
3 tbsp liquid glucose
1 vanilla pod, split lengthwise

1 In a bowl, whisk the egg yolks and sugar until thick and pale.
2 Put the milk, cream, glucose and vanilla pod in a pan and bring to the boil.
3 Pour slowly on to the egg-and-sugar mixture, whisking all the time, until smooth.
4 Return the mixture to a clean pan and heat gently, stirring constantly, until the mixture thickens to a custard. Be careful not to let the mixture boil.
5 Remove from the heat, leave to cool, covered with punctured cling-film to prevent a skin forming, then remove the vanilla pod and churn in an ice-cream maker according to manufacturer's instructions.

White Chocolate Ice-cream

Make as Vanilla Ice-cream, but omitting the vanilla pod and stirring 115 g white chocolate into the warm mixture until melted.

Rum and Raisin Ice-cream

Put 75 g raisins in a small bowl and pour over 3 tablespoons rum. Leave to macerate for 2 hours. Proceed as for Vanilla Ice-cream, omitting the vanilla pod but adding the rum and raisins to the warm mixture.

Coconut Ice-cream

Proceed as for Vanilla Ice-cream, omitting the vanilla pod and using coconut milk instead of ordinary milk. Pour 3 tablespoons Malibu into a pan, heat gently and then flame it carefully. When the flames have died down, add to the warm mixture.

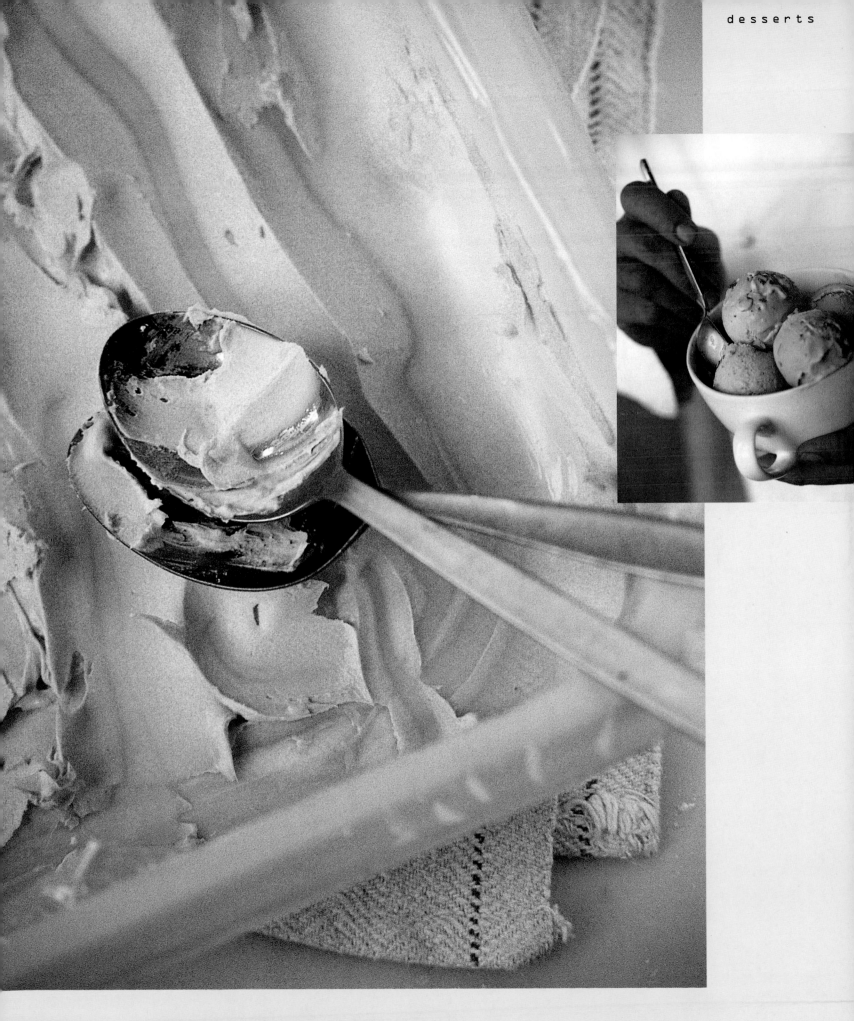

Strawberry Ice-cream

Purée enough strawberries to make 100ml. Proceed as for Vanilla Ice-cream, omitting the vanilla pod, using only 75g sugar and stirring the strawberry purée into the warm mixture.

Orange Sorbet

500 ml fresh orange juice
150 g unrefined caster sugar
100 ml liquid glucose

1 Put all the ingredients in a pan with 100ml water. Bring to the boil (the sugar will dissolve).
2 Remove from the heat and leave to cool. Churn in an ice-cream maker or sorbetière according to manufacturer's instructions.

White Chocolate Sauce

serves 6

4 egg yolks
40 g unrefined caster sugar
450 ml milk
40 g white chocolate, thinly sliced

1 In a bowl, beat together the eggs and sugar until pale and thick.
2 Bring the milk to the boil in a pan, then pour it over the egg-and-sugar mixture, stirring.
3 Place the bowl over a pan of simmering water and stir until the mixture reaches a sauce-like consistency. Remove from the heat.
4 Add the white chocolate and stir until melted and well mixed in. Pass through a fine sieve.
5 Allow to cool, covered with punctured cling-film to prevent a skin forming, then chill.

Caramel Ice-cream

Make a caramel sauce by putting 125 g unrefined caster sugar in a pan with 5 teaspoons water and heating gently until the sugar has dissolved and you have a golden caramel. Add 5 teaspoons boiling water (take care as there may be lots of steam and splashing) and stir in well. Proceed as for Vanilla Ice-cream, omitting the vanilla pod and stirring the caramel into the cooled mixture.

Calvados Pomme Verte Sorbet

500 ml apple juice
75 g icing sugar
5 tbsp liquid glucose
juice ½ lemon
drop of apple-green colouring (optional)
25 ml Calvados

1 Put the apple juice, icing sugar, glucose and lemon juice in a pan and bring to the boil (the sugar will dissolve). Remove from the heat and stir in the colouring if you are using it.
2 Heat the Calvados in a pan and then carefully set light to it, to flambé. When the flames have died down, add the Calvados to the pan containing the apple juice.
3 Leave to cool and then churn in an ice-cream maker or sorbetière.

Dark Chocolate Sauce

serves 6

125 g unrefined caster sugar
50 g good-quality cocoa powder
100 ml double cream

1 Put all the ingredients in a pan with 300 ml water, bring to the boil, then cook gently over a low heat until it thickens to pouring consistency. Pass through a fine sieve.
2 Allow to cool and chill as above.

Crème Anglaise

serves 4-6

3 egg yolks
25 g unrefined caster sugar
250 ml milk
½ vanilla pod

1 In a bowl, beat together the egg yolks and sugar.
2 Put the milk and vanilla pod in a pan and bring to the boil. Pour on to the egg-and-sugar mixture, stirring well.

3 Pour the mixture into a clean pan, return to the heat and cook gently, stirring, until the mixture thickens to a pouring consistency. Pass through a fine sieve.
4 Allow to cool as for the chocolate sauces opposite.

Coffee Sauce

serves 4-6

Make in the same way as Crème Anglaise, but add 1 teaspoon of ground coffee beans dissolved in a little boiling water.

Caramel Sauce

serves 4-6

250 g sugar

1 Put the sugar in a pan with 100 ml of water and heat gently until the sugar dissolves.
2 Continue cooking gently until you have a thick, golden caramel.
3 Remove from heat, pour in 100 ml of boiling water, taking great care as there will be lots of steam and splashing, and allow to cool.

Brandy Snap Baskets

The brandy snap mixture, like tuile, is pliable when it is warm and can be fashioned into any shape you choose: the classic way is to roll it up like cigars and then fill each one with cream. I like to mould the mixture into baskets in which we then serve desserts of fruit and ice-cream or sorbet.

makes 4

250 g unsalted butter
250 g unrefined caster sugar
250 g plain flour
1 tbsp ground ginger
250 g golden syrup

1 Preheat the oven to 180°C/350°F/gas 4.
2 Put the butter in a pan and melt gently. Reserve.
3 Put the sugar, flour and ginger into a food processor and begin to mix at low speed. Gradually add the golden syrup, followed by the melted butter and continue to process until all the butter is incorporated.
4 Divide the mixture into 4 rounds about 10 cm apart on a non-stick baking tray. Flatten each round with the palm of your hand, to form four 12-cm circles.
5 Bake in the oven for 5–8 minutes, until golden.
6 Remove the tray from the oven and leave to cool for a moment, until you can safely handle the brandy snaps. Press each one into a soup terrine or over-sized tea-cup and leave until cool and crisp. Turn out and use the 'baskets' for holding fruit and/or ice-cream.

bread puddings

Most cultures have a tradition of cooking with bread, born out of poverty, but humble puddings like the French *pain perdu,* or bread pudding, can also be elevated into something richer and more special — particularly if you use brioche as your base.

Brioche

As a child I used to walk past the local bakery and pâtisserie in the early morning. The windows were all lit up, you could smell the yeast, and there was an ambience and a buzz about the place. When I was fourteen I worked there part-time and since then I have never failed to be seduced by the aromas of bread straight from the oven.

However, a chef and a baker have different temperaments. A baker needs to be calm, relaxed and responsive to the dough; me, I am always impatient, I like a fast pace. When you try this recipe, do it when you have time and you are feeling relaxed. Once you have made it you can use it as we do in the restaurants, to make a luxurious pain perdu or bread and butter pudding.

If you want to make a whole brioche, rather than small ones, use a large tin and bake the brioche for 20-25 minutes. You could also use a food mixer with a dough hook.

makes about 16 small brioches

15 g fresh yeast, cut into small pieces
500 g plain flour, plus more for dusting
1 tbsp salt
45 g caster sugar
6 large eggs, beaten
200 g unsalted butter

for the glaze:

1 egg
pinch of salt
a little granulated sugar

1 Dissolve the yeast in a little warm water and leave for 5 minutes.

2 Sieve the flour and salt into a mixing bowl and add the sugar. Make a well in the middle, add the yeast and mix together well.

3 Beat in the eggs, a little at a time, until all the ingredients are completely incorporated. The dough should be still sticky, but not too soft.

4 Flour your hands, then knead the dough slowly and steadily for about 6 minutes, lifting it towards you with one hand (you can use a scraper to help), then flipping it back quite firmly on to the work surface. When you knead, put your whole body behind it, not just your hands. As you work, keep sprinkling flour on the surface and continue kneading until you have a dough which feels elastic and no longer sticks to your fingers.

5 Soften the butter to the same consistency as the dough, then spread it over the dough with one hand and knead it in with the other in the same way as before.

put a ball of dough in each. Cover with cling-film and leave in a warm draught-free place until doubled in size again.

8 Make the glaze: beat the eggs with the salt and glaze the brioche carefully.

9 Using a pair of scissors, make little cuts in the top of the brioche and sprinkle over a little granulated sugar.

10 Bake for 10-12 minutes until golden brown (do not open the door for the first 6 minutes, until the brioche have fully developed).

11 Remove from the oven and leave to cool on a rack.

6 When all the butter has been worked in, dust a large bowl with flour and put in the dough. Cover with cling-film and secure with an elastic band. Leave in a warm draught-free place, at 20-22°C/68-72°F, until doubled in size. Knock back.

7 Preheat the oven to 180°C/350°F/gas 4. Oil 16 brioche tins or muffin trays well (you can bake the brioche in batches if necessary) and

Pain Perdu

At home, when I was growing up, my mother often made this dessert with leftover bread and, sometimes, a little caramelized apple to go with it. I loved it then and I love it now. This is a slightly smarter version, with brioche, nuts and ice-cream.

serves 4

4 thick slices of Brioche (see previous page)
1 litre milk
175 g unrefined caster sugar
1 vanilla pod, cut lengthwise into 4 strips
175 g walnut halves
100 g pistachio nuts
100 g peeled hazelnuts
100 g sultanas
Vanilla Ice-cream (page 150), to serve

1 Dip the brioche briefly in the milk.

2 Put the sugar in a pan with 4 tablespoons of water and cook gently until the sugar has dissolved and you have a golden caramel. Add the vanilla strips.

3 Heat a frying pan and add a little of the caramel. Add the brioche and cook lightly on each side. Add the nuts and sultanas to the pan. Stir to coat.

4 To serve: place a slice of brioche in each of 4 serving dishes, pour on the rest of the caramel sauce and decorate with the nuts and sultanas. Add a scoop of vanilla ice-cream and garnish with a strip of vanilla.

Bread and Butter Pudding

To finish, a crazy Frenchman's version of a very English pudding. Of course, you do not need to spin globes of caramel for decoration or even add my trio of sauces... you can even use soft white bread rather than brioche (increasing the demerara sugar to 100 g), although the brioche just makes it a little richer... but why not end as I hope you began this book, in a spirit of adventure...

serves 4

100 g dried apricots, chopped

3 tbsp kirsch

100 g mixed raisins and sultanas

3 tbsp rum

about 40 g butter

1 dessert apple, peeled, cored and diced

3 tbsp Calvados

8 slices of Brioche (see previous pages)

1 tsp ground cinnamon

1 tbsp unrefined demerara sugar

300 ml milk

½ vanilla pod

2 eggs, plus 1 extra yolk

125 g unrefined caster sugar

for the stock syrup:

200 g unrefined caster sugar

for decoration (optional):

Crème Anglaise (page 153)

Dark Chocolate Sauce (page 152)

Caramel Sauce (page 153)

Caramel (page 17) spun free-hand into a globe
     shape rather than springs

the night before:

1 Make the stock syrup: put the unrefined
caster sugar in a pan with 600 ml water, stir to
dissolve and bring to the boil. Remove from
the heat. Pour half into a separate pan.

2 To one pan of stock syrup add the dried
apricots and kirsch. To the other add the
raisins, sultanas and rum. Boil up each pan,
then remove from the heat, cover and leave to
infuse overnight.

next day:

3 Preheat the oven to 180°C/350°F/gas 4.

4 Heat 15 g of the butter in a pan and sweat
the diced apple until just soft.

5 Add the Calvados and bubble up until the
contents of the pan are reduced to a purée,
and reserve.

6 Spread the brioche slices thinly on
both sides with butter and cut them into
cubes. Put into a bowl with the drained

apricots, raisins and sultanas, and the apple,
cinnamon and demerara sugar.

7 Put the milk and halved vanilla pod into a
pan and bring to the boil.

8 In another bowl, mix together the eggs, egg
yolk and caster sugar until pale. Pour the milk
slowly over the egg and sugar mixture, beating
all the time until smooth. Put through a fine
sieve and add to the bowl containing the

brioche and fruit. Stir to combine well.

9 Butter 4 dariole moulds and divide the
mixture between them.

10 Bake in a bain-marie in the preheated oven
for about 30 minutes, until golden brown and
well risen.

11 To serve: turn the puddings out of their
moulds and serve with the three sauces.
Decorate with spun caramel.

index

acknowledgments

To my spiritual brother Marco – thank you for your vision, support and help over so many years – and to my family, who gave me a good start. A big thank-you to all who have contributed to the making of this book – in particular: everyone at Quadrille, especially Mary Evans for her art direction; editor Lewis Esson and designer Paul Welti; Sheila Keating, a long-time friend who came up with the theme and helped turn my thoughts into words; and Jean Cazais, probably the only photographer who can make me laugh under pressure.

Special thanks to my PR, Maureen Mills of Network London, who helped bring me out of the shadows into the spotlight, with patience, humour and belief; and, among all the journalists who have supported me, Jonathan Meades – the first critic to single me out.

This book is not just about me, it is about a team, especially my loyal band of chefs/directors in the picture above who joined me from The Four Seasons to take a gamble on launching Maison Novelli: (from left to right, back) Jean-Marie Lenfant (Le Moulin de Jean, Brecey, Normandy), Mike Bird (Head Chef, Novelli W8), Richard Guest (Group Executive Chef), Duncan Impey (Group Pastry Chef), (front left) Nick Wilson (Head Chef, Les Saveurs de Jean-Christophe Novelli).

Also thanks to George Jardine (Executive Chef, Novelli at The Cellars, Cape Town), Jason Ward (Sous-Chef, Maison Novelli) and Chris Wheeler, my assistant, who has been like a brother to me, Igor Timchishin (Head Chef, Novelli EC1), my brother Anthony, Vicky Guest (Head of Reservations), Andy Phillips (Financial Director) and his team; Pascal Risso (Group Front of House Manager and design guru), Howard Linskey (Marketing and Operations Director), Jeanne Monchovet (Internal Public Relations), Xavier Chapelou (Group Wine Purchaser), Nikki Curtis (Personnel Manager), Ian Finnan, Dave Roberts and his team, and every single member of staff.

In the restaurant business good buying is fifty per cent of the success and I am lucky to have great suppliers, especially my long-time friend Bobby Lee at Daily Fish.

Thanks, too, to Liz McGrath, Fredrik Aspegren and all the team at The Cellars in Cape Town, my friends at SeaFrance and all my previous employers (even those who gave me the sack!), as well as the following people I have worked with or for, over the years: the Elie de Rothschild family, the old Chewton Glen team, especially Pierre Chevillard, Dominic Prandi, Alain Rocher; Denis Sirries, Gerard Basset, Giuseppe Vurchio, Neil Saunders, Nick and Sally Trant, Keith Floyd, Bill Stone, Fabrice Guihery, Robert Cole, Françoise Peretti and her team, Chris Watson, Per Redhead, Filip Tibos, Mike Ouchbakou, Chris Thompson, Ramon Pajares, Robert Cima, Karen Earp, Vinicio Paolini and his team, Rory Purcell, Nigel Firth, Colin Short, Jimmy Lahoud, Michele Andjel, Jon Gall and Jo Langridge from NatWest, Perry Lewis, Simone Kilka, Sarah Webb, Catey Hillier, Susan Duncan, David Pritchard, Yves Sauboua, Nick Grimshaw, Sarah Lewis, Claude Douard, Andrew Nurnberg, Trevor Hughes, Marcus Steel, Jean Louis Farjot, Olivier Poivre d'Avor, David Boland, Joachim Schafheitle and many more.

I have to thank God for giving me all my five senses, the people who helped me to understand how to use them, those who appreciate them, and those who join with me to try to use them to perfection – whether it is in the kitchen, in business, in love... on all parts of the planet. Success is based on where you stand today, not yesterday, not just where you came from, but where you are heading. I will always be proud to be French, but coming to Britain was my only chance to be myself, and I won't forget all the people whose company I have enjoyed and who have helped me on my way in this country – from the day I arrived with nothing but two suitcases and a packet of Gitanes. I believe success comes from a combination of elements: shared creativity, honesty, loyalty, respect and passion, so thanks to everyone who have helped and supported me personally and whose energy and hard work has contributed to the success of the Novelli Group. Above all, thanks to those who, through the best and worst of times, will still be my friends tomorrow. You know who you are and how I feel about you.

Finally, a big thank-you to all my customers. I will always have time for you!

A percentage of proceeds from this book will go to SOS Children and the Red Cross Hospital, Cape Town, of which I am a patron – not because I have a huge heart, but because those kids need help and they are the future.   JCN